LEARNING TAROT REVERSALS

LEARNING TAROT REVERSALS

JOAN BUNNING

WEISERBOOKS

Boston, MA/York Beach, ME

First published in 2003 by
Red Wheel/Weiser, LLC
York Beach, ME
With offices at:
368 Congress Street
Boston, MA 02210
www.redwheelweiser.com

Library of Congress Cataloging-in-Publication Data

Bunning, Joan.
   Learning tarot reversals / Joan Bunning.
     p. cm.
   ISBN 1-57863-271-4
   1. Tarot. I. Title.
BF1879.T2.B834 2003
133.3'2424--dc22

               2003014719

Typeset in 11/14.5 Centaur
Printed in Canada

10 09 08 07 06
 8 7 6 5 4 3 2

The paper used in this publication meets the minimum requirements of the American National Standard for Information Sciences–Permanence of Paper for Printed Library Materials z39.48–1992 (r1997).

To fools everywhere,

LEAGUE OF FOOLS

Why are you sitting in
   a darkened room,
     my friend?
To the window with you!
Spread wide those drapes.
Throw up that sash.
Lean way out and drink in
   great draughts of light.
Better yet,
Climb out on the ledge
   and raise high
     your precious cup.
Shout to the sun,
   "Bottoms up!"
Passersby will stare.
They will slap their thighs
   at you, the silly drunk,
     hanging by your heels.
But, be you still
   a tippler of the air.
Join the league of fools
   besotted by
     the potent wine of joy.

—JEB

CONTENTS

ACKNOWLEDGMENTS

I wish to thank Steve for his never-failing support and design of the figures in this book. Thanks also to David and Jonathan for keeping the household lively and fun while Mom toiled away at the computer. I would also like to thank the staff at Red Wheel/Weiser for their many contributions to this effort.

In addition, I wish to thank the tarot teachers, writers, and students who have shared their insights and experiences with me over the years. You've added tremendously to my understanding. Finally, I offer my heartfelt gratitude to those everywhere who have felt inspired to look within for their Inner Guides. You are making a difference in the world.

INTRODUCTION

The tarot is a set of seventy-eight intriguing picture cards that symbolize universal forces. A tarot reading involves selecting certain cards at random after shuffling and cutting the deck. When you examine these cards, you see how certain forces are impacting your life in the moment. You gain insight into your experience and access to the wisdom of your Inner Guide.

I became fascinated with the tarot during the 1980s. I discovered the cards are a powerful tool for personal and spiritual growth. As I worked with my deck, I gradually felt drawn to write about my experiences, to capture what I was learning about the intuitive process. Later I arranged these writings into a course.

In October 1995, I created the Learning the Tarot website, *www.learntarot.com*, built around my lessons. Over time, my online experiment grew into a full-time project. I still maintain my site, but now my course also exists as the book *Learning the Tarot: A Tarot Book for Beginners*.

Learning the Tarot covers the features of the deck, card meanings, and interpretation techniques, including one lesson on reversed cards (cards that are upside-down in a reading). This introductory lesson just touches upon the subject, which really deserves a book of its own. *Learning Tarot Reversals* is that book.

My approach to reversed cards is based on an appreciation of energies and their cycles. In our world, change is the one constant. A reading shows us forces that are not fixed, but fluid and dynamic. The cards need to reflect this animated spirit if they are to mirror experience faithfully. In *Learning Tarot Reversals*, I describe how card orientation is the key to enhancing the energetic quality of a reading. You can enliven and deepen your tarot practice by adding this new dimension to it.

The format of *Learning Tarot Reversals* is the same as that of *Learning the Tarot*. Each book has lessons with accompanying exercises followed by a card section. The card section in *Learning the Tarot* covers upright meanings. The card section in this book gives a brief review of upright meanings and then covers reversed meanings in depth. Both use the same keywords. Together, the two books provide a complete reference for individual card meanings.

If you're new to the tarot, I recommend starting with *Learning the Tarot* or a similar beginner's book or class. If you get hooked on the tarot, as so many of us do, you'll be eager and ready to learn more. *Learning Tarot Reversals* will then be a natural next step in your studies. If you already have tarot experience, you should be able to understand and adapt the ideas in this book to your own methods.

The best approach to *Learning Tarot Reversals* is to read all the lessons straight through to get an overview of the concepts. Then go back to the beginning and study each lesson in more depth, working through the exercises provided. The exercises will give you a chance to put the ideas into practice. You don't have to do all of them before continuing, but they do build on each other to some extent, so it's best to do the exercises in order.

My responses to the exercises are given at the back of the book. I call these responses "suggestions" rather than "answers" because I want to emphasize that there is no right or wrong approach to the tarot. Every reader sees the cards from a unique perspective, but by comparing your view to mine, you'll deepen your grasp of the concepts.

To truly reflect reality, a reading must capture life's movement and change. In this book, I describe how you can enhance the dynamic quality of your readings by seeing your cards as energies. You'll discover how to translate a stationary set of images into a moving picture of time's flow. It's my hope that *Learning Tarot Reversals* will give you a new way to view your life experience and a more powerful tool for understanding it through the tarot.

Part I:

LESSONS

LESSON ONE: ENERGY AND THE TAROT

Imagine a finished jigsaw puzzle. Looked at one way, it's a single object presenting a whole picture. Looked at another way, it's a collection of many objects—the pieces of the puzzle. The puzzle is *one* and *many* at the same time.

Now, imagine the pieces moving and changing. The overall dimension of the puzzle stays the same, but the picture doesn't. It's recreated anew in every moment. Our universe is like this puzzle. It is a single entity, but made up of countless changing "pieces." I call these pieces energies.

An energy is anything that can be named or identified. Energies enjoy a temporary existence in a certain form. They are born, live for a time, and die, all the while contributing to the eternal flow—the animating Spirit that sustains all energies.

All living beings are energies, as are all inanimate objects. Qualities or states of being are also energies—the energy of love or despair can be a palpable force with a life of its own.

Energies often coalesce into groups to form larger energies. Each of us is such a group. Our bodies are made up of cells and organs; our personalities are traits and tendencies; our moods reflect thoughts, feelings, and desires. A person is a veritable energy vortex! Every minute of the day, energies of all kinds are flowing in, around, and through us. Some are mild, some strong. Some are new, some old. Some are welcome, some not so welcome. How does this energy flow relate to the tarot?

Every card in the tarot deck represents a certain energy. A card's energy is not its energy as a physical object, but the *larger* archetypal energy it symbolizes. A card's energy is its meaning, but with an added sense of movement and change.

A reading you do for yourself is a snapshot of your personal energy configuration at that moment. The cards you pick are the energies that best reflect your situation at that time.

Just as a snapshot stops the action of a real scene, a reading freezes the flow of your life. But life goes on after a photo is taken, and so do the energies reflected in a reading. Two readings done one after the other rarely contain the exact same cards. The energy pattern changes, even in that short time.

In fact, you impact the energies in and around you simply by doing a reading! You alter the flow of events by examining them. This is why working with the cards is so powerful. A reading helps you become aware of the key energies at play in your life so you can work with them creatively. In the next lesson, we'll begin looking in detail at the nature of energy flow and its expression in the tarot.

Exercise 1.1: Feeling Energies in the Environment

Set aside a stretch of open time during which you imagine everything in your environment as a living energy with awareness. Try to feel the presence of whatever you interact with. See the two of you as equals encountering each other for a shared purpose. Don't analyze your experience at the time. Just go about your life as if this way of being is completely natural. Later, think about these questions:

- How did I feel during this exercise?
- Did this way of being change my interactions? How?
- Were some energies easier to feel than others?
- Did I notice any answering responses?

Exercise 1.2: Feeling Card Energies

Choose a card from your deck and look at it for a while. Keep part of your awareness on the card and part near the center of your chest, your heart area. This will help you "feel" rather than "think." If thoughts occur, gently set them aside and return to your meditation.

After a time, allow words to bubble up that capture the card's energy for you. Don't reach for words, just let them come. The words you receive will be unique to you. Repeat this exercise on other days. Some words will repeat, others will be new. Card energies adapt to changes in you and your environment.

Exercise 1.3: On What Do I Spend My Energy?

In his excellent book *The Teachings of Don Carlos* (Bear & Co., 1995), Victor Sanchez talks about the body as a field of energy. He suggests a number of techniques to enhance our energy bodies. One is making an inventory of energy expenditures. Here is an abbreviated version of this exercise:

1. Divide a notebook page into three columns with these headings:

What was I thinking?
What was I doing?
Is this what I want to do?

2. Set a portable alarm or watch to go off every thirty minutes. Don't set it for the hour or half-hour, as you don't want to anticipate the alarm.

3. For one day, whenever the alarm goes off, answer the above three questions in regard to that moment, writing your responses in your notebook. Don't analyze. Just make a short notation, right away, in the moment.

4. At the end of the day, review your comments, looking for recurring elements and patterns. Note the relationship between your thoughts and actions. How often were you doing what you really wanted to do?

5. Continue this exercise for a week or even a month. At the end of each longer period, do #4 again, covering that greater stretch of time.

6. The goal is observation of yourself, so answer honestly. You want to know what energies are truly active in your life—and they're not necessarily the energies you think!

LESSON TWO:
THE ENERGY CYCLE AND ORIENTATION

Take a moment to become aware of your breathing. Feel how your chest expands as you inhale deeply. You fill your lungs, pause for a moment, and then exhale. Your chest slowly contracts as you breathe out.

This is the pulse of life. It's how energies flow within ourselves and our world. A wave builds, peaks, and crashes to the shore. Anger flares up and dies down. Civilizations rise and fall. Figure 1 (below) shows this universal energy cycle—how an energy starts low, builds to a peak, and then fades over time.

When you do a reading, the cards you draw represent energies important to you at that moment. Each one is at a certain point in its individual cycle. One may be strong, another weak. One may be on the rise, another fading. To understand the reading, you need to know the status of each energy—where it is in its cycle.

The orientation of a card gives you this information. Orientation is the direction a card faces on the reading surface (or as you hold it). A card can be upright (normal view) or reversed (upside-down). Usually orientation is obvious, but not always. Sometimes cards are slanted or horizontal in a reading. You need to decide ahead of time how you will interpret these cards for orientation.

Figure 2 (below) shows the energy curve with a horizontal line dividing it in half. The section above the line covers the period when an energy is strong—at or near its peak. The section below the line covers those periods when an energy is weak—either just beginning (left) or ending (right).

We can now relate card orientation to energy in this way: An upright card represents an energy in the part of its cycle above the line. A reversed card represents an energy in the part of its cycle below the line.

Figure 1   *Figure 2*

The energy curve as an island.

Upright cards stand for energies that are strong and well-developed. They have a clear, active presence. You recognize their impact in the situation. Reversed cards stand for energies that are absent, weak, or undeveloped. They are not clear and obvious. You can't easily recognize their presence for the moment.

For example, an upright World would imply happiness is strongly present. You feel pleased with life and quite fulfilled. A reversed World suggests a lower level or unrealized happiness—for now.

An energy does not become its opposite when reversed. A card's essential nature stays the same no matter what its orientation. A reversed World does not show active unhappiness (the opposite of happiness). It shows the energy of happiness is low—a subtle difference! True unhappiness has its own active energy and might appear in a reading as a card such as the Nine of Swords.

Imagine the energy curve as an island viewed from the side (see illustration, above). The horizontal line is the surface of the water. Above the surface is the part of the island we can see; below the surface is the part we can't see. Although this part is hidden, it's still present.

Sometimes a reversed card represents an energy that is hidden, rejected, or ignored. It's not available because it hasn't yet "come to the surface." An upright Devil might show an obsession you acknowledge; a reversed Devil, one you deny. A denied obsession is unconscious, but very real.

A reversed energy can also be at a low level because it's new and tentative—in the early part of its cycle—or because its almost gone—approaching the end of its cycle. In both cases the energy is weak, but for quite different reasons. In the next lesson, we'll take a detailed look at these phases to see what they can tell us about the energies in our lives.

Exercise 2.1: Noticing Energy Cycles

Become aware of energy cycles in your experience. Notice when one first appears. It may be a feeling, thought, person, or event. Follow the energy as it develops over time. Watch it gain and lose power as it goes through its cycle.

See if you can detect when an energy is peaking. At a group event, you can sometimes feel the exact moment when the group's energy has reached its crowning moment. As always, avoid intellectual analysis. Concentrate on how an energy feels as you experience it.

Exercise 2.2: Is the Energy Present or Lacking?

For each item below, say whether the specified energy is actively present or lacking based on the accompanying statement. Also give the orientation that would best match that energy status. (See Suggestions for Exercises on page 159 for possible responses.)

Example: Energy = Relationship
"I haven't been in a relationship for two years."
Response: Relationship is lacking = reversed

1. Energy = Fitness
   "I'm in the best shape ever right now."
2. Energy = Depression
   "I'm depressed all the time these days."
3. Energy = Compassion
   "I don't feel sorry for him; he knew what he was doing."
4. Energy = Greed
   "I don't want much, just what's fair."
5. Energy = Pride
   "I'm clearly the best candidate; the others don't have a chance."
6. Energy = Attraction
   "There isn't much of a spark between us."
7. Energy = Sorrow
   "I'm not sad about what happened; it had to be."
8. Energy = Devotion
   "I'd do anything to help my daughter get well."
9. Energy = Creativity
   "I haven't come up with a new idea in months."
10. Energy = Denial
    "I'm not denying involvement."

Exercise 2.3: Lacking vs. Opposing Energies

For each item below, say which of the two statements shows a lacking energy (absent or weak), and which shows an opposing energy, and name the opposing energy. (See Suggestions for Exercises on pages 159–160 for possible responses.)

Example: Energy = Love
#1 = "I absolutely can't stand that man."
#2 = "My love for him is almost gone."
Response: #1 = Opposing (hating)
#2 = Lacking (not in love)

1. Energy = Enthusiasm
   #1—"I'm not too enthusiastic about the idea."
   #2—"I reject the idea."

2. Energy = Self-reliance
   #1—"I depend on my family for everything these days."
   #2—"I'm not as independent as I'd like to be."

3. Energy = Honesty
   #1—"I didn't say exactly what I was thinking."
   #2—"I lied."

4. Energy = Practicality
   #1—"That plan is not workable yet."
   #2—"That plan is completely crazy."

5. Energy = Humor
   #1—"That story didn't get any laughs."
   #2—"That story made me cry."

6. Energy = Achievement
   #1—"I failed."
   #2—"I'm no longer doing very well."

7. Energy = Sacrifice
   #1—"I'm going to take that position for myself."
   #2—"I'm not ready to give up my position."

8. Energy = Running Away
   #1—"I won't go until you're feeling better."
   #2—"I'll stay with you forever."

9. Energy = Weariness
   #1—"I'm full of vitality."
   #2—"I'm not so tired after that good night's sleep."

10. Energy = Imagination
    #1—"The orders spell out exactly what to do."
    #2—"The orders don't leave much room for creativity."

LESSON THREE:
ENERGY PHASES

In the last lesson, you learned about energy cycles and orientation. Figure 3 (below) shows how a cycle is made up of three distinct phases—early, middle, and late.

Each phase has its own unique character:

Early-phase energy is just beginning. It's not yet developed, but it's growing. It's moving toward full expression in the future.

Middle-phase energy is strong and developed. It's clear, immediate, and obvious in the present.

Late-phase energy is on the decline. It's losing power and clarity. The energy's full expression is in the past.

An upright card represents an energy in the strong, middle phase of its cycle (above the line). Interpreting upright cards is fairly straightforward because there's only one possible phase. The energy is well-developed, active, and near full strength.

A reversed card is not so easy to identify because its weak energy can be in either of two phases: early or late (below the line). You can tell which one by looking at how the card fits into the overall situation.

The best clue comes from an awareness of timing. A reversed card is in the early phase if you haven't really experienced its energy as yet. It may be new, or tied to some upcoming event. A reversed Five of Swords is in the early phase if you know you're heading into some contest or battle.

A reversed card is late phase if you've already experienced its energy. It's been active in the situation in a way you can easily recognize, but it is now past. A reversed Five of Swords is in the late phase if you've gone through some battle that is now winding down.

You can also identify phase by sensing the "feel" of an energy. Is it growing or fading? A growing energy is developing, expanding, or moving toward you. You sense it's going to get stronger and

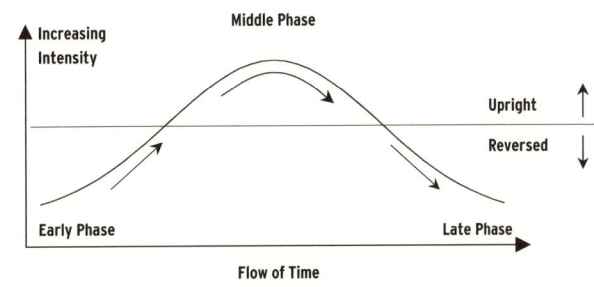

Figure 3

more noticeable. A fading energy is contracting or moving away. It's getting weaker and less noticeable.

The reversed Knight of Wands can represent a low level of passion. The passion is early phase if you feel it's going to get stronger and more compelling. It's late phase if it's lost most of its drive and power.

Sometimes a reversed card shows an energy that's absent. Its level is so low that, to all intents and purposes, it doesn't exist. But, appearances can be deceiving! If a card appears in a reading, you can assume its energy is playing some kind of role. The energy may be so new, you can't perceive it yet. It may only seem absent because you're unconscious of it, but it's still having an impact.

Let's look at how you might interpret one reversed card's energy. I'll use the Five of Pentacles as an example. The keyword meanings for this card are Hard Times, Ill Health, and Rejection.

If the Five of Pentacles is upright, you know its energy is in the middle phase of its cycle. It's strong and developed. You might be in debt, out of a job, sick, or suffering a rejection. These are all obvious instances of the energy of hard times in the present.

If reversed, the Five of Pentacles energy is either absent, weak, or undeveloped. If no hardship comes to mind, it may indeed be absent for the moment, but you should still be on the alert! You may be getting sick, but don't know it because there are no symptoms. You may think you're unconcerned about money, but an unconscious fear of poverty is affecting you nonetheless.

If you can identify a hardship, but it's not yet strong or active, the energy's in the early phase. Perhaps you've heard rumors of layoffs, but no one has yet been let go. Maybe you've had some minor chest pains, but you've been ignoring them.

If you've already experienced a hardship, the energy is in the late phase. It's passed through your life. If you were laid off, that would be a major difficulty that's now behind you. If you've been having serious money problems, you can guess they're now going away.

Knowing an energy's phase can help you deal with the energy effectively. You can anticipate what to expect knowing where the energy is in its cycle.

In the next lesson, we'll see how energy cycles tend to repeat themselves.

Exercise 3.1: Which Phase?

Decide whether the energy of each event below is in the early, middle, or late phase of its cycle, and say why. Also give the orientation that matches that phase. (See Suggestions for Exercises on page 161 for possible responses.)

Example:	**Event = Arriving at a party**
Response:	**Early phase = reversed**
	Your experience of the party is just beginning.

1. Handing in a finished test
2. Watching the opening scene of a movie
3. Saying goodbye to a friend
4. Giving a talk you've been preparing for months
5. Seeing your child off on the first day of school
6. Reaching the top of a mountain you've been climbing
7. Returning from a week's vacation
8. Preparing the soil of your garden in early spring
9. Being served the main course of a meal
10. Saying your vows at your marriage ceremony

Exercise 3.2: Growing or Fading Energy?

For each item below, decide whether the given energy is growing or fading based on the accompanying statement. Find a tarot card to represent that energy. You can use the keyword lists and card description pages for guidance. (See Suggestions for Exercises on pages 161–162 for possible responses.)

Example:　　**Energy = Anguish**
　　　　　　　"I seem to by crying more and more these days."
Response:　**Anguish is increasing = Nine of Swords**

1. Energy = Relationship
   "Breaking up was hard, but I'm getting over it."
2. Energy = Restriction
   "Every day I feel more trapped in my dead-end job."
3. Energy = Prosperity
   "Sales are really improving these days."
4. Energy = Diligence
   "She's working harder to get the job done."
5. Energy = Hope
   "I'm starting to feel we can make this relationship work."
6. Energy = Truce
   "The chance for a truce is slipping away."
7. Energy = Trust
   "I no longer trust my friend because she lied to me."
8. Energy = Apathy
   "One day I'm not going to care whether she leaves or not."

9. Energy = Competence
"Our team keeps getting better."

10. Energy = Downfall
"It's becoming less likely she'll be removed from office."

Exercise 3.3: Which Card Fits?

For each item below, place the three cards listed in front of you in the given orientation. Decide which one best reflects the energy of the statement, and say why. You can use the keyword lists and card description pages for guidance. (See Suggestions for Exercises on page 00 for possible responses.)

1. "I'm #1 in the rankings. No one can beat me now."
    a. upright Six of Wands
    b. upright Temperance
    c. reversed Nine of Wands

2. "I just can't tell my mother how I feel about her interference."
    a. reversed Six of Pentacles
    b. reversed Queen of Swords
    c. reversed Hierophant

3. "I'm not ready to contact my family yet."
    a. reversed Ten of Cups
    b. upright Five of Swords
    c. upright Ten of Pentacles

4. "I'm so glad that crisis is behind me."
    a. upright Death
    b. reversed Tower
    c. reversed King of Wands

5. "I love being a new mother."
    a. upright Page of Swords
    b. upright Empress
    c. upright Ten of Wands

6. "There's a slight chance I'll meet someone at the party tonight."
   a. upright Hanged Man
   b. reversed Moon
   c. reversed Ace of Cups

7. "Thank goodness that picky editor has quit. He drove me crazy with his obsessive changes."
   a. upright Knight of Swords
   b. reversed Knight of Cups
   c. reversed Knight of Pentacles

8. "I had a chance to change direction, but now it's disappearing."
   a. upright Sun
   b. reversed Seven of Pentacles
   c. reversed Strength

9. "I feel so lonely right now separated from everyone."
   a. upright Three of Swords
   b. reversed Nine of Swords
   c. reversed Wheel of Fortune

10. "I'm not prepared to hear the news. I just don't want to face it."
    a. reversed Eight of Wands
    b. upright Two of Swords
    c. upright Seven of Swords

Exercise 3.4: Fill in the Blank

Spread all the cards face down in front of you. Shuffle, and pick one at random. Look at the card while maintaining its orientation.

If the card is upright, say the following out loud:
   I am _____ right now.
If the card is reversed, say one or both of the following out loud:
   I'm not yet _____, but I will be in the future.
   I'm no longer _____, but I was in the past.

Fill in the blank with the first word or phrase that comes to mind as you respond to the card image. Repeat this exercise with as many cards as you wish.

This exercise can lead to some interesting insights. What does the meaning you chose say about you and your life? Notice any mistakes, hesitations, or changes you make "by accident."

Exercise 3.5: Phases of a Card's Energy

Pick a card to work with. Using the Five of Pentacles example in the text as a model, imagine the energy of your card as you might experience it in each of the three phases—early, middle, and late. Try to come up with several possible scenarios in each case.

LESSON FOUR:
REPEATING CYCLES

Energies don't begin and end abruptly. They flow in waves. When we finish one breath, we begin another. A love affair ends, but a new one begins. Each instance is unique, but the pattern repeats.

Figure 4 (below) shows an energy cycle repeating as time passes. We can capture this flow by bringing the ends of one cycle together to create a circle. The cycle is now an ever-spinning wheel. (see Figure 5). In the tarot, the Wheel of Fortune represents this circular pattern of energy at the cosmic level. This card is the model for all the smaller energy cycles we experience personally.

It's helpful to look for repeating energy cycles in your life so you can encourage the positive ones and avoid the negative. The best time to affect a repeating cycle is when the energy is low—in the early or late phase. Once a cycle is in full swing, the energy is strong and hard to change. In this lesson, I'll describe how the repeating nature of energy affects reverse card interpretation.

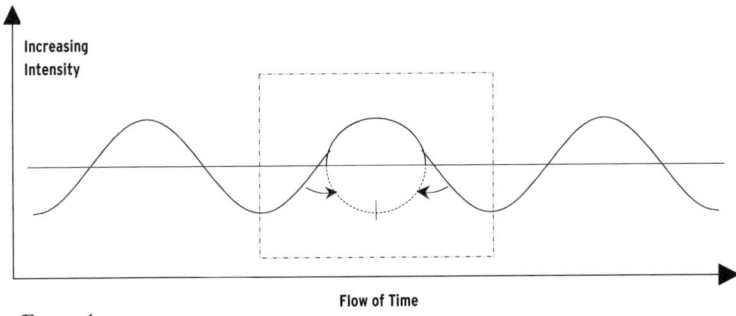

Increasing Intensity

Flow of Time

Figure 4

Middle Phase

Upright

Reversed

Early Phase   Late Phase

Figure 5

Early Phase

An early-phase energy is just developing, but you can experience it as either new or repeating.

A first-time energy has a fresh quality. You respond to it spontaneously. It can be delightful or unnerving, depending on the energy. The past is not dictating your responses, but you also don't have experience to guide you.

A repeating energy is familiar. It triggers old patterns. Your responses are more predictable, but also more assured. Assumptions from the past color your experience, but you have more knowledge to go by.

Sometimes you can experience an energy as if for the first time even though it's familiar. You deliberately let go of the past and greet the energy as new. Let's say you've drawn the Nine of Cups reversed. This card can show a possible sensual encounter in the future. The event may be new or one you've enjoyed before. In either case, it will be more delightful treated as a first!

You can also recognize a pattern that is starting to repeat, and change your habitual response. Awareness helps you break the pattern. The Nine of Swords reversed can show a worry beginning to trouble you. If you recognize that worry, you can choose to avoid old thought patterns if they are not helping.

To figure out if an early-phase energy is repeating, ask yourself the following questions:

- Is this energy familiar?
- Have I been in this situation before?
- Are my reactions predictable?
- Do I feel compelled to act in certain ways?
- Is it hard for me to change my behavior?
- Can others predict my actions?

Late Phase

Late-phase energy is fading, but you can experience it as complete or incomplete.

A completed energy brings peace and closure. You can let go with little doubt or hesitation. You know the energy has been resolved, so you can put it to rest.

An incomplete end is only temporary. The energy is going to return to be resolved. Sometimes an energy fades because it has been neglected or mishandled. Sometimes the timing wasn't right for it to continue. Such energies will likely rise again at a more opportune moment.

A reversed Justice can show the approaching end of a legal matter. If the case isn't resolved to your satisfaction, you may feel the need to start the cycle again. Or, you can decide to accept the ruling and move on.

To figure out if a late-phase energy is incomplete and thus likely to repeat, ask yourself the following questions:

- Am I dissatisfied with what's happened?
- Do I feel compelled to hold on?
- Is something keeping me from releasing?
- Am I sorry this energy is fading?
- Was this energy cut off prematurely?
- Will I want to revisit this energy again?

Knowing energy tends to repeat helps you appreciate the subtle shifts that occur at the reversed card stages. You can watch for past influences affecting new energies. You can make sure fading energies are resolved satisfactorily.

You now have a basic understanding of the energy cycle and its reflection in the tarot. In the next lesson, we'll start expanding on that knowledge. I'll describe what you can learn when a card's orientation doesn't match your expectation.

Exercise 4.1: New or Repeating Energy?

Each item below gives a reversed card and the early-phase energy it might represent. Decide whether the energy is brand new or repeating based on the statement. If the energy is repeating, list a few possible assumptions from the past that might be coloring the situation. (See Suggestions for Exercises on pages 163–164 for possible responses.)

Example:	**Reversed Wheel of Fortune**
	Energy = Major direction change
	"I think management's going to change direction again. I hate when that happens."
Response:	**Energy of major direction change = repeating**
	Possible past assumptions:
	Management always messes up.
	Change is always negative.
	New directions never work out.

1. Reversed Queen of Pentacles
    Energy = Trust
    "I'm not sure I should trust her again, she's lied to me so often."
2. Reversed World
    Energy = Realizing your dream
    "I've never been within sight of my dream before."
3. Reversed Ten of Pentacles
    Energy = Financial security
    "For the first time in my life, I can imagine being free of money worries."

4. Reversed Ten of Swords

Energy = Feeling like a victim

"I've never felt like a victim before."

5. Reversed Two of Pentacles

Energy = Fun

"I always have fun at that resort. We'll have a blast next week."

6. Reversed Ace of Wands

Energy = Confidence

"Every time I start to feel confident, something knocks me down."

7. Reversed Emperor

Energy = Organization

"I've never been organized before. This new system may just work."

8. Reversed Seven of Swords

Energy = Hidden dishonor

"The president asked me to hide those payments again. I think I have to do it."

9. Reversed Hanged Man

Energy = Letting go

"I don't know how to let go, but I may have to try."

10. Reversed Page of Cups

Energy = Forgiveness

"He called last night, but I didn't answer. I'm not going to forgive him this time.

Exercise 4.2: Complete or Incomplete Energy?

Each item below gives a reversed card and the late-phase energy it represents. Decide if this ending feels complete or incomplete based on the statement, and give a reason. (See Suggestions for Exercises on page 164 for possible responses.)

> **Example:**   **Reversed Two of Wands**
> **Energy = Originality**
> **"No one accepted my new ideas, but I'm not going to give up."**
> **Response:**   **Energy of originality = Incomplete**
> **The desire to realize an original vision is still strong.**

1. Reversed Four of Swords

Energy = Rest and recovery

"That quiet weekend did the trick. Now I'm rested and ready to go."

2. Reversed Ace of Pentacles

   Energy = Prosperity

   "Our sale was a hit, but I'm glad everything's back to normal."

3. Seven of Cups

   Energy = Wishful thinking

   "I realize it was just a fantasy, but I can't help thinking about it still."

4. Reversed High Priestess

   Energy = Mystery

   "Maybe the case's been closed, but I won't be satisfied until I know the truth."

5. Reversed Three of Cups

   Energy = Friendship

   "It was great to see my old friends at the reunion last week."

6. Reversed Moon

   Energy = Fear

   "I'm not afraid now that he's gone, but if he comes back, I'll be terrified."

7. Reversed Page of Wands

   Energy = Courage

   "It took courage for me to jump out of that plane but one sky dive is enough."

8. Reversed Chariot

   Energy = Hard control

   "I don't force my son to do his homework any more. We've worked out a more cooperative arrangement."

9. Reversed Lovers

   Energy = Sexuality

   "I can't accept being friends after we've been lovers for so long."

10. Reversed Queen of Cups

    Energy = Love

    "My grandmother loved me so much. I can't accept that she's rejecting me now."

Exercise 4.3: Noticing Repeating Cycles

Examine your life for repeating cycles. Are there any patterns that seem to recur over and over? When such a pattern begins, check for assumptions you are bringing forward from the past. Are there any patterns you were able to resolve successfully? Think about how you were able to break free of the repetition and move forward.

LESSON FIVE:
MISMATCHES

We humans have an endless capacity to fool ourselves. We misperceive motivations and actions. We read into a situation what we wish were true and fail to recognize tough realities we would like to deny. This is why the tarot is such a valuable tool. The cards act as a mirror reflecting truths about our experience. They let us know when our perceptions are not aligned with the energies of the moment and our own best interests.

When a card's orientation matches your expectation, you can feel fairly confident you are seeing your situation realistically. But what if a card's orientation doesn't match? If you think a card should be facing one way, but it's facing another, you have an excellent opportunity to become more aware!

A general rule of thumb is: When a card's orientation doesn't match your expectation, you're misperceiving the strength of the card's energy.

Card Is Reversed, You Expect Upright

If you feel a reversed card should be upright, you're experiencing that energy as stronger than it really is. You're giving it more weight than is justified for the moment.

Sometimes an energy is absent when you believe it's present. Or the energy is not yet as developed as you think. It may be in the early phase, but you see it as further along in its cycle:

> You've been preparing diligently for a major exam, but you draw the Nine of Wands reversed. The fact that this card appeared at all shows that perseverance is relevant, but the reversal implies you're not working hard enough. You need to step up the pace if you want to succeed.

Sometimes a reversed energy is no longer as strong as you think. It's moved to the late phase, but you still see it as active:

> You did a reading about a major game your team lost and drew Judgement reversed. Your coach was critical of your performance at the time. You thought he was still judging you harshly, but the reversal tells you otherwise. His negative opinion has been much reduced.

Card Is Upright, You Expect Reversed

If you feel an upright card should be reversed, you're underestimating the strength and presence of the energy. It's having a more immediate impact than you realize:

> You and your partner have been trying to adopt a child. None of your attempts have worked, so you're about to give up. You're surprised and delighted when you draw the upright Six of Cups. This card often represents a baby. The upright orientation tells you something concrete is happening even though you don't yet know what it is.

Sometimes you think an energy is almost gone, but it's actually still in play. You may not be aware of the effects, but they're real nonetheless:

> You've drawn the Ace of Swords in a reading about your youngest child. This card sometimes shows a challenge testing you in some way. You recognize the challenge, but you thought you'd resolved the problem. The upright orientation tells you it's still active!

You can see from these examples how a card's orientation offers a way to catch misperceptions and denials. The tarot reflects energy patterns without bias or judgment. The cards show you the reality of a situation. It's up to you to accommodate that truth.

In the next lesson, we'll look at how orientation works with card pairs.

Exercise 5.1: Actuality vs. Belief

Each item below gives a card and an energy it represents. (See Suggestions for Exercises on pages 165–166 for possible responses.) In each case, give the following:

1. Describe the actual strength of the energy based on the card's orientation.
    Upright = strong; Reversed = weak
2. Describe the belief about the energy's strength based on the statement.
3. Is there a match? If not, what's the misperception?

Example:	**Energy = Faith**
	Card = upright Fool
	"I've lost almost all faith in myself."
Response:	**Faith is actually strong (card is upright)**
	Faith is believed to be low (lost all faith)
	No match
	Misperception = Faith is stronger than it seems.

1. Energy = Travel

   Card = upright Six of Swords

   "I'm traveling all the time these days."

2. Energy = Aggression

   Card = upright Seven of Wands

   "I'm not really mad at my landlord, even though he raised my rent without warning me."

3. Energy = Attention to detail

   Card = reversed Eight of Pentacles

   "I checked my application ten times. It's got to be correct."

4. Energy = Romance

   Card = reversed Knight of Cups

   "We don't enjoy many romantic moments now that the baby's here."

5. Energy = Moderation

   Card = reversed Temperance

   "I'm living a quiet, moderate life these days. I never overindulge."

6. Energy = Recognition

   Card = upright Sun

   "No one remembers my achievements. I've been forgotten."

7. Energy = Quiet contemplation

   Card = reversed Four of Cups

   "I need to meditate more frequently, but I can't seem to find the time."

8. Energy = Leadership

   Card = reversed Three of Wands

   "I'm a good leader. My team respects my example."

9. Energy = Fairness

   Card = upright King of Swords

   "That judge has a reputation for being honest and fair."

10. Energy = Attraction

    Card = upright Two of Cups

    "He's not attracted to me at all. He'll never ask me out."

Exercise 5.2:

Choose some cards from the deck either randomly or by group, such as all the major arcana or court cards. If you're ambitious, use all seventy-eight cards!

On a piece of paper, mark off three columns with the following headings:

Energy / Perceived Strength / Actual Strength

Fill in the first two columns for each card. In the first column, write one energy the card represents to you right now. In the second column, say whether you perceive that energy as strong or weak at this time in your life.

Shuffle the cards you picked, and hold them face down in your hand. Turn them over one by one. In the third column, write the actual strength of the card based on its orientation: upright is strong, reversed is weak.

Compare the two columns and answer these questions:

1. How often was there a match?

2. Do the mismatches have a common feature?

3. Was I surprised by the orientation of certain cards?

4. Did the outcome seem random or meaningful to me?

LESSON SIX:
OPPOSING ENERGY PAIRS

One day you feel the urge to go on an adventure. You drive to a new beach, explore for a while, take a swim, and return home, tired and happy. The next day you venture out again, but this time your trip's a disaster. Your car breaks down, and you cut your foot on a shell. You give up all thoughts of adventure and decide to explore the joys of your living room. You've traded adventure for security.

Energies come in linked pairs that are opposites: hot/cold, hard/soft, adventure/security. In lesson four, you learned that energy cycles often repeat. It's also common for energies to switch back and forth between their opposites. Figure 6 (below) shows the relationship between any two opposite energy cycles. The top circle represents the single energy pattern we've been working with so far. Now, a second cycle is linked to it.

Let's see how the beach trips fit into this pattern. Your first trip began in the energy of adventure (top cycle). You initiated a trip and then returned home—one successful turn around the circle. Because the trip was fun, you stayed in the energy of adventure and repeated the cycle the next day.

This time the trip was not fun, so you left the energy of adventure and moved to the energy of security (bottom cycle). Your unpleasant adventure led you to seek the opposite. If the appeal of security stays strong, you may remain in the security cycle for a while. Or you may forget your bad trip at some point and desire adventure again.

In the tarot, linked energies are represented by two cards with opposite meanings. Some cards are natural opposites such as the Fool and Death. The Fool stands for beginnings and Death for endings. Aces and court cards can also be opposites. The emotional Queen of Cups and practical Queen of Pentacles are poles apart in some circumstances.

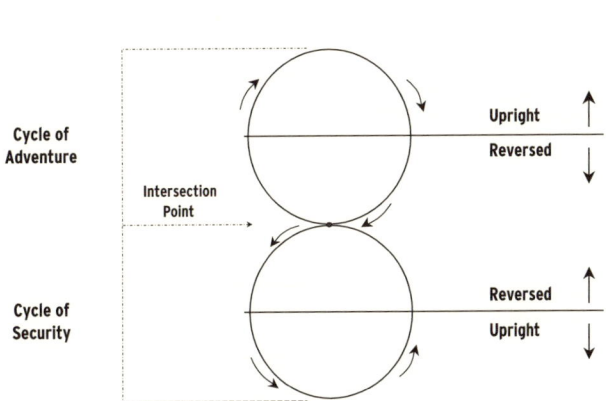

Figure 6

Sometimes the energies of two cards are linked temporarily in a certain situation. They're not normally opposites, but have that relationship for a time. Let's say you do a reading about a deadline and draw the Nine of Wands and Two of Pentacles. The Nine might show the tough perseverance you need to finish in time. The Two might then show a contrasting desire to have fun.

Once you've identified two cards in a reading as an opposing pair, the orientation of the cards can help you understand their relationship. Notice how in Figure 6 the two cycles come together in the reversed phases. An energy must fade before it can shift to its opposite. If an energy is strong and clear (upright), its as far away as possible from its opposite.

Let's look at how to interpret opposing card pairs by orientation. Here are two basic principles:

If the cards in a pair have the same orientation, their energy levels are roughly equal.

If the cards in a pair have different orientations, the upright energy is the stronger one.

Both Cards Are Upright

When opposing cards are upright, their energies are both strong. This can mean struggle and tension. It's difficult to keep two contrary tendencies in play at the same time. You may be absorbed in one, while someone is resisting you from the other. Or you may be trying to balance both tendencies in yourself simultaneously. The upright Ten of Wands paired with the upright Seven of Swords can show a struggle between wanting to meet responsibilities (Ten) and wanting to run away from them (Seven).

Both Cards Are Reversed

If opposing cards are reversed, the situation is flexible. At some level, you're exploring both energies before committing. Little may seem to be happening, but you're setting your future. It's a time of opportunity. A reversed Two of Wands and a reversed Eight of Swords can indicate an unclear power issue. Feelings of power (Two) and powerlessness (Eight) are trading off with neither one dominant.

One Card Is Upright, One Reversed

Different orientations show a swing in progress. You're shifting from one energy to the other. If the reversed energy is growing (early phase), it's on its way to replacing the upright energy. The upright Six of Wands (pride) and reversed Tower (downfall) pair is a perfect symbol for the saying, "Pride goeth before a fall!"

Sometimes a reversed card shows an energy that is absent compared to its upright opposite. In this case, the reversed energy is at the intersection point (see figure 6). It's not developed, but it's present as a possibility. The reversed Tower in the above example might be a hint that the "seed" of some humbling fall has been planted in the situation.

If you sense a reversed energy is fading (late phase), it's being replaced by its upright opposite. A reversed World paired with an upright Five of Wands can show that the spirit of cooperation (World) is giving way to competition (Five).

The orientation of two court cards can show the energy balance between two people. Let's say the King of Wands and King of Pentacles represent you and your partner in a reading. If these cards have the same orientation, you are both at *about* the same energy level. If one court card is upright and one reversed, there's an energy imbalance—one of you is "stronger" than the other in some way related to the situation.

Working with card pairs helps you understand the action of opposing energies in your life. In the next lesson, we'll talk about how orientation can expand your understanding of groups of cards.

Exercise 6.1: Matching Opposing Pairs

Below are two scrambled lists of pairs. The pairs in the left column are opposing energies. The pairs in the right column are opposing cards. For each energy pair on the left, find the card pair on the right that most closely matches. You can use the keyword lists and card description pages for guidance. (See Suggestions for Exercises on page 167 for possible responses.)

Enthusiasm, Apathy	Star, Devil
Resting, Quick Action	Sun, Eight of Cups
Mother, Father	Two of Wands, Ten of Pentacles
Materiality, Spirit	Four of Wands, Four of Cups
Hope, Hopelessness	Ace of Pentacles, Ace of Cups
Solitude, Relationship	Empress, Emperor
Guilt, Innocence	Four of Swords, Eight of Wands
Vitality, Weariness	Hermit, Lovers
Winning, Losing	Nine of Swords, Six of Cups
Originality, Convention	Six of Wands, Five of Cups

Exercise 6.2: Interpreting Opposing Pairs

Each item below has two opposing card energies. Interpret the two cards together, taking into consideration their given meanings and strengths. There are many possible interpretations. (See Suggestions for Exercises on pages 167–168 for possible responses.)

Example: **Reversed Six of Cups = low level of good will**
                  Upright Nine of Wands = high level of defensiveness
Response: **There is much defensiveness in the situation (upright Nine of Wands), but also**
                  a chance for some good will to develop (reversed early phase Six of Cups).

                  There was much good will in the past, but now it's gone (reversed late phase
                  Six of Cups). Some disillusionment caused the good feelings to be replaced
                  by defensiveness (upright Nine of Wands).

1. Upright Ace of Swords = high level of mental force
    Upright Ace of Cups = high level of emotional force

2. Upright Four of Pentacles = high level of structure
    Reversed Seven of Cups = low level of dissipation

3. Reversed Magician = low level of action
    Upright High Priestess = high level of nonaction

4. Reversed Six of Swords = low level of the blues
    Reversed Two of Pentacles = low level of fun

5. Upright Three of Wands = high level of foresight
    Upright Two of Swords = high level of avoidance

6. Upright Chariot = high level of hard control
    Upright Strength = high level of soft control

7. Upright Nine of Pentacles = high level of self-reliance
    Reversed Three of Pentacles = low level of teamwork

8. Reversed Empress = low level of abundance
    Upright Five of Pentacles = high level of hard times

9. Reversed Ten of Cups = low level of joy
    Reversed Three of Swords = low level of heartbreak

10. Reversed Fool = low level of spontaneity
    Upright Ten of Wands = high level of burdens

Exercise 6.3: Court Card Stories

Remove the sixteen court cards and place them face down on the table. Mix them well, and choose any two at random. Place them side by side, being sure to maintain the orientation.

Now make up a situation involving these two as imaginary characters. Say your story out loud. Describe each character and their interaction. Don't plan your story, just say the first impressions that come to mind.

The only "rules" for this exercise are:
- Kings and Queens are adults of any age.
- Knights are teens or adults.
- Pages are babies or young children.

Each character's personality must reflect the card's energy.

Orientation shows a character's strength or influence on the situation.

You are free to elaborate as much as you like. The ideal is to move beyond the exercise to feeling you really know these people and their situation.

Example:	**Energy Upright Queen of Cups**
	Reversed Page of Wands
Response:	**This woman (Queen of Cups) is the mother of this little boy (Page of Wands). Normally he's very lively and confident (Wands), but something upsetting happened at school. He's lost his usual enthusiasm (reversed late phase Wands). However, the mother has a handle on the situation (upright). She's very gentle and loving (Cups) and understands what her son needs. She'll be able to restore his self-assurance through her patient understanding.**

Exercise 6.4: Multi-Person Court Card Variation

This exercise is a variation of exercise 6.3 for two or more people. Each person chooses a card (without showing it to anyone else). One person begins by establishing an improvisational scene as a character matching his or her chosen card. Other people react from their own card characters. Follow the rules of age, personality, and strength. When the scene has played out, everyone can try to guess which cards were drawn by the others.

Exercise 6.5: Opposing Energies in Life

Become aware of the play of opposing energies in your life. As you go about your daily activities, notice how often energies come in pairs, one force balancing another. Can you sense how the lessening of one energy corresponds to the growth of another (though not always immediately)? Keep a small notebook handy to jot down energy pairs as they occur to you. Look for examples both within and without. You will find them everywhere.

LESSON SEVEN:
ENERGY GROUPS

In the last lesson, you learned how upright and reversed energies work within opposing pairs. Orientation is also meaningful for groups of cards. A group is any set of cards with a common characteristic. In a reading, you can determine the energy status of a group by comparing the number of upright and reversed cards in it.

Usually there is a mixture, showing balance in the group's energy. Some forces are strong and developed, some are not. When there is balance, orientation is not too significant.

It's rarer for all (or nearly all) cards to have the same orientation. This gives the group a definite energy character. When the cards are all upright, the group energy is strong and well-developed. When reversed, the group energy is weaker and less developed. The larger the group, the more pronounced the effect.

Let's see how orientation works with different card groups:

Major Arcana

The major arcana cards are potent archetypes with extra force and impact. If they are all upright in a reading, their energies are near maximum strength. Together, they make a powerful group indeed. If they are all reversed, that strong effect is damped down.

Let's say you draw the Chariot, Moon, and Empress in a three-card reading. Getting three out of three major arcana cards is striking enough, but if they are all upright, they make a very potent group. The overall energy level is high. If the cards are all reversed, the group energy is suppressed. The effect is not as strong as it could be.

Court Cards

Many court cards in a reading can suggest the involvement of many people. The combined group effort is creating a strong energy. If all the court cards are reversed, people are more hesitant and uncertain. The energy of the situation is low because people are not participating fully.

Suits

Each suit represents a different element and approach to life:

Wands (fire)—passion, action, risk-taking
Cups (water)—love, emotion, intuition, trust
Swords (air)—intellect, truth, justice
Pentacles (earth)—material world, money, practicality

If all the cards of a suit are upright, that suit's quality in general is well-developed in the situation. If reversed, it's less developed. For example, if the cups in a reading are all reversed, the energy of love and emotion is absent or at a low level.

Spread Groups

A spread is a pattern for laying out the cards. Card groups are built into the design of many spreads. The cards in these groups are usually placed together physically. Such a group can be devoted to a person, event, location, or time period. The orientation of the cards in the group defines its energy level. For example, some relationship spreads have two groups of cards that mirror each other—one set for each person. If all the cards in a group are the same orientation, you know much about that person's overall energy level and engagement in the relationship, at least at the time of the reading.

Spontaneous Groups

Certain cards in a reading can strike you spontaneously as a group. The orientation of those cards describes the energy state of whatever feature brings the group together. Let's say you've drawn the Sun, Three of Cups, and Four of Wands in a reading. You notice these cards of high spirits are all reversed. Even though each one has its own individual meaning, as a group the three cards suggest that celebration is at a low level. Joy in general is suppressed for some reason.

The Entire Reading

The distribution of upright and reversed cards in a reading describes the energy of the entire situation. An uneven distribution shows a definite energy state.

If all cards are upright, the situation is well-developed. Abundant energy is available. Actions are being taken, or the time is right for action. There are few hidden agendas or unrecognized problems. The focus is on the present, not the past or future. The situation is straightforward, open, and obvious.

A reversed reading is less developed. The overall energy is low. There is little momentum toward goals. Actions, if any, are low-key and tentative. Much is unexpressed or unexposed. The focus is on the past or future, not the present. On the other hand, the situation is flexible. New directions are possible because choices have not been fixed. People have not yet committed. There is opportunity for change.

You can apply an understanding of orientation to good effect at all levels of a reading. In the next lesson, we'll put everything together into a strategy you can use to interpret both upright and reversed cards.

Exercise: Intuitive Scanning

This exercise will help you develop the ability to get an overall impression of a reading before you begin looking at individual cards. Repeat the exercise often until intuitive scanning and assessment comes naturally.

Shuffle and cut your deck, and lay out some cards in the spread of your choice. Scan the reading lightly for card orientation. Try to get an impression of the distribution of upright and reversed cards without slipping into detailed analysis. You want to "sense" the energy levels in groups and in the reading as a whole.

When you're done, reinforce your efforts with some feedback. Draw a diagram of your spread, and color in the card "squares" by orientation: dark for upright, light for reversed. You can now see energy strengths at a glance.

Next, fill in the following chart. You may also find this diagram and chart useful when doing your personal readings.

Group Category	Total Number of Cards in Group	Number of Upright Cards in Group	Number of Reversed Cards in Group
Entire Reading	_____	_____	_____
Major Arcana	_____	_____	_____
Court Cards	_____	_____	_____
Wands	_____	_____	_____
Cups	_____	_____	_____
Swords	_____	_____	_____
Pentacles	_____	_____	_____

LESSON EIGHT:
INTERPRETATION STRATEGY

You now have all you need to begin working with reversed cards. In this lesson, I'll describe a strategy you can use to get to any card's core meaning, whether upright or reversed. This method will help you integrate orientation into your tarot practice. I'll present the whole technique first, then take you through an example.

Step 1: What's the card's energy?

Get an impression of the card's energy—its meaning to you at the time of the reading. Many meanings are possible. As always with the tarot, much depends on your awareness and intuitive responses in the moment. Three elements are important:

Traditional meanings
Personal meanings
Your response to the image

Step 2: What's the context for this card's energy?

Place the card's energy within a context. Context comes from three main sources:

Your situation at the time of the reading
Your question, if any
The spread position meaning, if any

Step 3: How strong does this card's energy feel to me?

Assess your experience of the energy. Which description below fits best?

Strong , present, developed, obvious, active
Weak, absent, undeveloped, hidden, inactive

Step 4: Does my feeling (step 3) match the energy's actual strength (orientation)?

Compare your experience of the card's strength to its actual strength based on orientation. There's a match if an upright card's energy feels strong to you, or a reversed card's energy feels absent or weak.

If there's a mismatch (Lesson 5), review the above steps again. Take another look at your idea of the card's energy, context, and strength. Try to discover what it is you may have missed.

Step 5: What is the energy's phase (reversed cards only)?

Figure out where a reversed energy is in its cycle (Lesson 3).

Absent—energy does not seem present at all
Early—energy is somewhat present, but strong phase lies ahead
Late—energy is somewhat present, but strong phase is past

Step 6: Is this a repeating energy?

Assess whether or not you've experienced this energy before (Lesson 4) . If you can recognize a repeating pattern, you can make more informed choices, especially in the early phase. If there is a late phase energy, does it feel complete or incomplete?

Step 7: Are there any opposing energies?

Check for other cards with opposing energies. Consider the effect of orientation (Lesson 6). Suggestions for opposing card pairs are given in *Learning the Tarot*.

Step 8: Is the card's energy part of a group?

See if the card belongs to any groups (Lesson 7). Check suit and type (major arcana, number, or court card). Is the card in a position grouping? Does it seem linked to certain other cards? How does it fit into the reading as a whole?

Step 9: What do I want to do about this energy?

Once you understand a card's energy, you can decide what to do about it. You can encourage, discourage or simply let the energy be. The choice is up to you!

• • •

These are the steps for a single card. You can repeat them for all the cards in a reading. With each pass, your interpretation will shift a little, but gradually you'll build up a solid understanding of all the energies and their relationships.

Example

You decide to do a reading about a problem at work. This week your manager told you she wants you to inform her daily about your progress on a certain project. You think this monitoring is a waste of time. You told her you'd rather inform her voluntarily, but she still insists.

You do a reading to answer the following question: "What do I need to understand about the disagreement I'm having with my boss?"

You draw the reversed Four of Pentacles in the "key feature of the situation" position.

Step 1: What's the card's energy?

Three traditional meanings for the Four of Pentacles are possessiveness, control, and blocked change. In the past, this card has often meant control to you. You see the figure as trying to hold down the coins. He seems to be saying, "You're not going anywhere without my permission!" So, you settle on the control meaning for now.

Step 2: What's the context for this card's energy?

The situation is anything related to your interaction with your boss—both internal and external. Your question narrows the focus down to what "you need to know to better understand the disagreement." The position meaning suggests control is a *key feature*.

Step 3: How strong does this card's energy feel to me?

You believe your boss is definitely trying to manage your work. You feel control is a strong and obvious aspect of the situation.

Step 4: Does my feeling (step 3) match the energy's actual strength (orientation)?

If the card were upright, you would have a match. You feel the energy is strong (step 3) and upright cards show strong energies. Because the card is reversed, there is no match. You think the control is obvious, but the reversal suggests otherwise. You wonder why the level is low. For now, you're willing to accept the possibility that you may be overestimating the control.

Step 5: What is the energy's phase (reversed cards only)?

You rule out late phase because your manager's request is new. Early phase seems best, but you wonder if the control may actually be absent—a radical thought!

Step 6: Is this a repeating energy?

You have to acknowledge this scenario feels very familiar. You always get angry and defensive at any hint of control. Are you setting yourself up for another round of charges and counter-charges?

Step 7: Are there any opposing energies?

You check for cards with opposite energies, such as the Hanged Man (letting go) or the Fool (being spontaneous and free). You also look for cards that reinforce the idea of control, such as the Emperor (authority) or Chariot (hard control).

Step 8: Is the card's energy part of a group?

You look at the other pentacles cards and their locations. Is the Four of Pentacles in a special position group? Can you intuitively link this card with any others?

Step 9: What do I want to do about this energy?

You still feel there's a element of control in this situation, but you're also willing to consider the possibility that it may be pretty low. You decide to talk to your manager calmly to find out what her goals are. Then, maybe you can work out an arrangement that will work for both of you.

Your review of the Four of Pentacles led to an unexpected insight. You realized you *may* have introduced the control energy into this matter yourself, perhaps because of past experiences. If control does turn out to be a growing feature of this situation, you now have a deeper awareness of the dynamics involved.

• • •

As you can see, these steps offer one way to discover the meaning of a card's energy. This approach is anaytical, but only at first. As you practice with it for a time, your interpretations will become more profound and integrated. In the end, you'll have a trustworthy method for tapping into the wisdom of your Inner Guide.

Exercise: Getting to the Core Meaning

Try the strategy in this lesson the next time you feel a one-card reading would be helpful. Decide on a position meaning for the card and also write a question about your concern. Some possibilities are:

- What are the fundamental issues at stake?
- What do I most need to consider?
- What is the most likely outcome?

Now draw one card and place it in front of you. Be sure to maintain the orientation. Follow the interpretation strategy step by step. When you're used to the procedure, you can try this approach on all the cards in a full reading.

The benefit of a strategy is that it helps you avoid floundering during interpretation. You have a way to approach each card that leaves you with a useful understanding. The disadvantage is that a strategy tempts you to abandon your intuition to rely on a rote system. You don't want your interpretation to become automatic.

Practice with this procedure for a while, but don't come to depend on it. Always trust your intuitive responses first.

AFTERWORD

In sacred geometry, there's a pattern known as the seed of life. It's said to represent the most basic processes of life. The seed of life is made up of six symmetrical circles touching at a central point with a seventh circle defining the center.

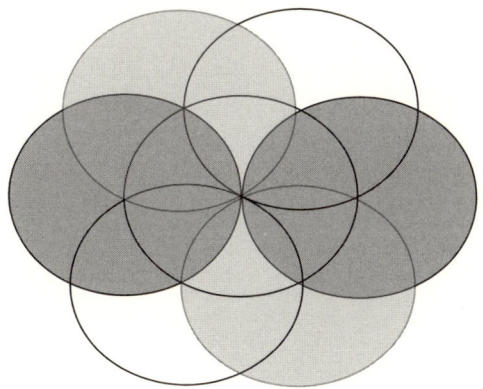

Figure 7

Notice how this figure is made up of three different opposing energy pairs. Imagine expanding this symbol to include an infinite number of such pairs, all arising from the same point.

In essence, we are this stillpoint center. Our lives are made up of the energies we choose to live and express in the eternal moment. We hold within ourselves all possible energy choices.

When you work with the tarot, you not only gain insight into your daily life, but you have the chance to develop a certain serene perspective on your own experience. As energies come and go, you begin to realize that your fundamental nature is not that precious chaos. Your spirit lies much deeper than the ebb and flow of those passing tides.

When we view our lives from a little distance, we can feel the poignant beauty of the play of energy without getting drawn away from our center. To be able to flow with energies without drowning, to meet each tide with love and gratitude, is truly to be centered.

I hope these lessons have deepened your appreciation of the energies of life as expressed within the tarot and your own experience.

Part II:

REVERSED
CARD DESCRIPTIONS

This section gives reversed meanings for each card as well as a short summary of the upright meaning. Meanings are given as a series of short statements. I chose the short-statement format for this book to supplement the detailed upright card descriptions in *Learning the Tarot*. The statements are simply suggestions to help you get a sense of the reversed energy for each card.

Many statements are directed toward you, as in:

"You're not completing a task."

Others are general or directed toward someone else:

"The journey is not beginning."
"Someone is no longer rejecting love."
"People may come together soon."

I offer these possibilities for variety's sake. Feel free to adapt any statement to fit your circumstances.

The statements for each phase reflect the nature of that phase. Absent energy is not present, so these statements are always in the negative:

"You're not in a relationship."
"You have no stamina."
"You're denying your destiny."
"There's little justice at the moment."

Early phase energy may develop in the future, so statements suggest what *may* happen:

"You may start exploring options."
"A delay may develop."
"You may become strong in the future."

Late phase energy references the past. Statements show decline or events that have already occurred:

"Your power is fading."
"Someone is less obedient now."
"You've gone through a fateful encounter."

When interpreting a reversed card, read over all the statements given. Look for those that trigger the strongest response. Also, allow yourself to move beyond the statements given to others that are similar. You're not limited to what's written. Adopt a mood of waiting to see what pops into your mind. Often the ideal statement for the occasion will come to you spontaneously. If you get stuck, use the interpretation strategy described in Lesson 8.

MAJOR ARCANA

THE FOOL

Upright

It's a time of beginning. New paths and directions are available. Spontaneity is important. You can live in the moment with trust. Your faith is strong. Everything is unfolding as it should. What appears to be folly is not.

Reversed

Keyword: Beginning

Absent: You can't begin right now. A new direction is not available. People are not willing to explore the unknown. It's not the right time to start a journey. You're not able to take that first step.

Early Phase: You're getting ready to start. The journey may be about to begin. A new phase may be coming up. You're thinking of initiating a novel plan. The unknown may beckon.

Late Phase: The chance to begin is disappearing. The new opportunity is no longer available. The initiative is less likely now. The start date has passed. The unknown is losing its appeal.

Keyword: Spontaneity

Absent: There's little spontaneity right now. People are not feeling carefree. Impulsive behavior is rare. You're not living in the moment. There are few surprises. No one is breaking the routine.

Early Phase: The atmosphere may become freer. You may let go of expectations. It may get easier to act on the spur of the moment. You may start to feel more uninhibited.

Late Phase: The carefree times are ending. You're no longer willing to improvise. Impromptu decisions are less effective now. Someone is becoming less impetuous. The free and natural mood is fading.

Keyword: Faith

Absent: You lack faith right now. You don't trust the flow. It's not easy to feel sure. Your sense of security is not strong. Confidence is low. You don't have much hope.

Early Phase: Your faith may return. It may get easier to believe. You may gain more confidence. The situation may start to feel secure. Someone may become more willing to believe.

Late Phase: You're losing faith. Hope is fading. You're not as confident as you were. Someone is no longer trusting. The time of innocence is past.

Keyword: Apparent Folly

Absent: You're not willing to take a "crazy" chance. You don't trust what your heart is telling you. You're afraid to look foolish. Someone is not supporting your "silly" dream. Outrageous behavior is no longer accepted.

Early Phase: You may start to pursue a dream. You may become involved in some foolishness. You're getting ready to take a wild chance. You may decide to go for it, even if you fail.

Late Phase: The time to be wild and crazy has passed. You're more disillusioned now. It's no longer possible to pursue your dream. A bit of foolishness is behind you.

THE MAGICIAN

Upright

It's a time of action. You can do what needs to be done. Having conscious awareness is important. Your concentration level is high. Total commitment is possible. Power is available. You can make a strong impact.

Reversed

Keyword: Action

Absent: You can't take action right now. You're unable to maneuver. Plans can't be implemented. Your talents are not being used. There's not much happening. The work is not getting done.

Early Phase: The time for action may be approaching. You're getting ready to make your move. The plan may be going forward. You may have a chance to do what you have to do. There may be more activity in the future.

Late Phase: The time for action is ending. The activity level is decreasing. There's less support for your exploits now. Someone is using less force. People are no longer carrying out the plan.

Keyword: Conscious Awareness

Absent: You don't know what's going on. Someone is clueless. You're not sure of your motivations. The situation is not clear to you. True intentions are not being expressed.

Early Phase: You may begin to catch on. You may grow more aware. The true nature of the situation may become clear. People may start to speak openly. You may need to stay on top of things in the future.

Late Phase: You're becoming less aware. You're no longer sure what's happening. Your clarity of purpose is disappearing. It's not as easy to defend your position now. Understanding is fading.

Keyword: Concentration

Absent: You can't concentrate. You're not focused. There's no singleness of purpose. It's hard to stay centered. People lack commitment. Someone is off-message.

Early Phase: You may start to concentrate better. It may get easier to stay focused. Your sense of purpose may return. Dedication may grow. You may begin to commit to your goal.

Late Phase: You're no longer able to avoid distractions. Your commitment is not as strong. People are less dedicated now. The period of concentration is ending. Your energies are no longer focused.

Keyword: Power

Absent: You lack power at the moment. Your vitality is low. You're not having the impact you desire. You can't accomplish your goals. Energy is not available. Vigor is lacking.

Early Phase: You may become more powerful. You may start to make your presence known. Strength may increase. Your influence may grow. Potency may return.

Late Phase: Your power is decreasing. You're no longer as vigorous. The ability to sway the group is fading. Someone's prestige is declining. There's less energy available.

THE HIGH PRIESTESS

Upright

It's a time of nonaction. Events are unfolding on their own. Unconscious awareness is a factor. Your knowledge runs deep. There is great potential in the situation. Mystery is present. All is not being revealed.

Reversed

Keyword: Nonaction

Absent: You can't be inactive right now. It's not easy to stay calm. Being passive is not an option. You resist having to wait. Someone can't stay uninvolved.

Early Phase: You may begin to withdraw. You may have to lay low for awhile. A quiet time may be approaching. You may be idle in the future. Someone may start to show more patience.

Late Phase: The time of nonaction is ending. You can no longer stand by and watch. You're less inclined to remain passive now. The waiting is over. People are no longer willing to be quiet.

Keyword: Unconscious Awareness

Absent: Your intuition is not working. You're not listening to your inner voice. Unconscious material is not available. Dreams are hazy or hard to remember. Deeper realities are inaccessible.

Early Phase: You may begin to look within. Someone may open to inner truths. Unconscious material may start to surface. You may become aware of different realities.

Late Phase: You're no longer exploring the unconscious. Doors to the inner realms are closing. People are less willing to face hidden truths. It's getting harder to hear your inner voice. Interest in other realities is fading.

Keyword: Potential

Absent: You're not aware of the possibilities. You're denying a talent. Someone is not enabling growth. There's little recognition of potential. People are refusing to consider an opportunity.

Early Phase: You may begin to recognize your potential. A talent may develop. People may open to what could be. The possibilities may get clearer.

Late Phase: Your potential is no longer being recognized. The latent possibilities were not realized. People are less open to growth now. A talent is fading. An opportunity has passed.

Keyword: Mystery

Absent: You're avoiding a mystery. What's hidden is not being revealed. No one is looking past the obvious. There's little interest in the unknown. Someone is covering up a secret.

Early Phase: A mystery may come to light. You may start to look at what's been concealed. You may approach a closed-off area. Someone may be on the point of remembering. The unknown may beckon.

Late Phase: You're moving away from the mystery. The secret has been revealed or covered up. Someone has opened up a can of worms. Interest in the unknown is fading. The shadow-side is less exposed.

THE EMPRESS

Upright

It's a time of mothering and nurturing. Abundance is everywhere. There is more than enough for all. Senses are heightened. It's possible to give and receive pleasure. Nature is a vital part of the situation.

Reversed

Keyword: Mothering

Absent: You can't be a mother right now. Giving birth is not possible at the moment. Someone is not nurturing. There's a lack of tenderness. A mother is distant. A child is not connected to someone who cares.

Early Phase: Mothering may become more important. A birth may be approaching. A desire to nurture may grow. You may start to care for someone. A link with a child may come up. A mother may become more involved.

Late Phase: A time of mothering is ending. A birth has past. There is less nurturing now. A mother is not as close. You're becoming separated from a child. The feeling of being cherished is fading.

Keyword: Abundance

Absent: There's a lack of abundance now. Extravagance is not possible. A lavish reward is not in the picture. You can't indulge in luxuries. The path to riches is blocked. Someone feels there is not enough.

Early Phase: You may start to experience more abundance. An ample supply may be forthcoming. You may move toward plenty. There may be more than enough in the future. A surplus may become possible.

Late Phase: The time of profusion is past. People can no longer be extravagant. Wealth is decreasing. There is less to go around now. The coffers are emptying.

Keyword: Senses

Absent: You can't enjoy your senses. Someone is not vibrantly healthy. There's a lack of earthiness. Pleasure is being blocked. One of the senses is not working properly. Physical activity is low. Beauty is not being valued.

Early Phase: You may start feeling more sensual. Pleasure may become more important. Your vigor and energy may return. One of the senses may improve. You may start to focus on your body.

Late Phase: An experience of pleasure is past. You're no longer enjoying your senses. Physical activity is declining. There's less interest in the body now. One of the senses is failing.

Keyword: Nature

Absent: You're not involved with nature right now. Concern for the environment is not strong. Natural ways are not being embraced. You're out of harmony with natural rhythms. There's little connection with Mother Earth.

Early Phase: A relationship with nature may develop. You may start to feel more natural. Environmental protections may increase. Being outdoors may become more important. An experience with nature may occur in the future.

Late Phase: You're no longer involved with animals or plants. A focus on the environment is decreasing. People are feeling less connected with the Earth. There's less support for a natural approach.

THE EMPEROR

Upright

It's a time of fathering. It's important to provide direction. The focus is on structure. A coordinated plan is in place. Authority is an issue. Someone is concerned with control. Regulation and the law are involved.

Reversed

Keyword: Fathering

Absent: You can't be a father right now. Some connection to a father is broken. Someone is not offering security. You're not setting direction for a child. You're not defending someone in your care.

Early Phase: Fathering may become more important. You may begin to provide support. You may develop a connection to a child. A relationship with a father may improve. Someone may start to guide growth.

Late Phase: A time of fathering is ending. You're no longer supporting a child. A father is becoming less involved. The need for protection is decreasing. Being head of the family is no longer an issue.

Keyword: Structure

Absent: There's a lack of structure now. No one is following a plan. Coordination is low. You're not organized. People are not being systematic. Order is being disrupted.

Early Phase: Order may return. A plan may begin to take shape. You may start to coordinate activities. The environment may become more structured. Loose ends may be tied up in the future.

Late Phase: The structure is falling apart. Organization is declining. You're no longer following a plan. The period of order is ending. Fixed relationships are breaking up.

Keyword: Authority

Absent: You don't have authority right now. Someone is not showing leadership. There's a lack of command. Someone is not respected. No one's in charge.

Early Phase: You may start to exert control. An authority figure may become involved. Direction may be imposed. Respect may grow. You may have a chance to become a leader.

Late Phase: You're no longer in authority. You're losing your position of strength. Control is passing to someone else. Leadership is no longer strong. Officials are stepping aside.

Keyword: Regulation

Absent: Rules are not being followed. Standards of behavior are not in place. No one is regulating the system. Law and order is lacking. The regimen is not being followed.

Early Phase: You may begin to establish rules. A legal matter may become important. Contacts with the law may increase. Regulations may be enforced.

Late Phase: A legal matter is being concluded. Rules are decreasing. The monitoring period is over. There's less support for the program now. Regulations are no longer respected.

THE HIEROPHANT

Upright

It's a time of education. The pursuit of knowledge is important. Belief systems are having an influence. Traditions are in place. There's a spirit of conformity. Everyone is doing what's expected. A group identity is primary.

Reversed

Keyword: Education

Absent: You can't pursue learning right now. You don't have a chance to study. Someone is not in school. You're having trouble staying informed. Knowledge is hard to come by.

Early Phase: You may begin your studies. Someone may enter school. A thirst for knowledge may grow. You may need more information. A learning session may be about to start.

Late Phase: A time of learning is ending. Your studies are over. Getting an education is no longer a priority. You found out what you needed to know. Understanding is decreasing.

Keyword: Belief Systems

Absent: You lack a belief system. You're rejecting tradition. You don't want to proceed with a ceremony. People are not respecting their heritage. You don't know where to put your faith.

Early Phase: You may be forming a world view. You're getting ready to follow a discipline. A ritual may be coming up. You may decide to learn a set of beliefs. Traditions may become more important.

Late Phase: You're losing your beliefs. The traditional ways are no longer appealing. A way of life is disappearing. Your faith has been shaken. The old assumptions are less valid.

Keyword: Conformity

Absent: There's a lack of conformity. No one is following the rules. You can't fit in. Someone won't do what's expected. It's hard to adapt to the system. You're not ready to acquiesce.

Early Phase: You may begin to go along with the program. You may start to be more conventional. People may become more orthodox. Someone may fall in line in the future.

Late Phase: There's less conformity now. People are no longer abiding by the rules. The need to blend in is decreasing. The party line is losing its appeal. Someone is less obedient.

Keyword: Group Identification

Absent: You don't identify with a group. You're not joining an organization. The team is not together. There's little loyalty to the group. Someone is not committed to a communal effort.

Early Phase: You're thinking of joining a group. You may become part of a team. A spirit of community may be forming. Like-minded people may start coming together. You may decide to add your voice to others.

Late Phase: You're separating from a group. The time of togetherness is ending. Your commitment to the mutual cause is fading. The team is dissolving. There's less commonality.

THE LOVERS

Upright

It's a time of relationship. You can establish bonds and make connections. Sexuality is important. Passions are strong. Personal beliefs are influential. You can make up your own mind. It's time to consider values and ethical choices.

Reversed

Keyword: Relationship

Absent: You're not in a relationship. A marriage or union is not happening. It's not easy to make a connection. There is little intimacy. Kinship ties are broken. Someone is lacking love. Bonds are weak.

Early Phase: You may begin a relationship. Love may grow. A connection may develop. You may be drawn closer to someone. A marriage or union may occur in the future.

Late Phase: A relationship is ending. There's less intimacy now. You no longer feel love for someone. A family tie is loosening. Communication is decreasing. A partnership is dissolving.

Keyword: Sexuality

Absent: There is little sex right now. Desire is low. You can't express your passion. You're not attracted to someone sexually. Making love is not an option.

Early Phase: You may begin to feel a sexual attraction. Desire may grow. You may become more passionate. Life-force energy may increase. A sexual relationship may be initiated in the future.

Late Phase: There are few opportunities to be sexual now. You're losing your desire. The passionate phase is ending. The atmosphere is no longer sexually charged. The life-force energy is not as strong.

Keyword: Personal Beliefs

Absent: Your personal beliefs are not solid. You can't decide for yourself. It's difficult to know where you stand. Someone is not accepting your opinion. You can't challenge the entrenched system.

Early Phase: You may begin to think for yourself. You may come to your own conclusions. Someone may question the group consensus. A maverick thinker may get involved.

Late Phase: Your personal views are no longer involved. Your belief system has been challenged. The chance to make up your own mind is ending. It's harder to stay true to yourself at this point.

Keyword: Values

Absent: Values are not a high priority right now. You're avoiding an ethical choice. Someone is not staying true to ideals. Standards are not being met. No one is focused on what's right.

Early Phase: You may become more concerned with values. A moral or ethical dilemma may come up. You may have to choose between right and wrong. You may rediscover your ideals.

Late Phase: A code of ethics is no longer in place. Values are being discarded. Integrity is less of an issue now. The moment of temptation has passed. Your struggle with your ideals is ending.

THE CHARIOT

Upright

It's a time of victory. A triumph is in the air. Your will is strong. You can accomplish any goal. There's a need for self-assertion. Someone's interests are at stake. Powerful impulses are involved. Hard control is an issue.

Reversed

Keyword: Victory

Absent: You're not achieving a victory. The win is not happening. Someone is not beating the competition. The goal is not in sight right now. Domination is not possible.

Early Phase: You may begin to be successful. A victory may become possible in the future. You may triumph in the end. The path to the top may begin soon. A mood of conquest may develop.

Late Phase: The victory is behind you. Your string of wins is ending. A moment of triumph is in the past. You're no longer dominating. The battle is winding down.

Keyword: Will

Absent: You lack the determination to succeed. Your will is not strong right now. Self-discipline is low. Someone lacks willpower. The desire is not there. Your resolve is weak.

Early Phase: You may start to get focused. Your determination may grow. The desire for success may become stronger. Someone may show more discipline.

Late Phase: Your concentration is decreasing. You can no longer sustain an effort. The will to achieve is fading. You're less intent now. Your strength of purpose is weakening.

Keyword: Self-Assertion

Absent: You're not asserting yourself. You're not putting yourself forward. People don't know who you are. There's little need to be first. Your actions are not ego-based.

Early Phase: You may become more assertive. You may start to stand up for yourself. Self-confidence may grow. You're getting ready to ask for what you want.

Late Phase: You're less assertive now. You're no longer making your presence felt. Your desire to be first is decreasing. Selfish needs are losing importance. It's no longer necessary to grab the attention.

Keyword: Hard Control

Absent: There's a lack of hard control. Discipline is not effective. Someone is not maintaining order. Authority is missing. You're not keeping a lid on your feelings. You're not embracing the tough approach.

Early Phase: Strong controls may begin to be implemented. You may need to be firm in the future. Strict measures may become necessary. You may start to master your emotions.

Late Phase: The rigid controls are loosening. You're no longer in control. The reins of power are slipping away. The need to be strict is decreasing. You're putting an oppressive environment behind you.

STRENGTH

Upright

It's a time for strength. You can endure and thrive. Patience is important when dealing with frustration. There is room for compassion and sympathy. Soft control is effective now.

Reversed

Keyword: Strength

Absent: You're not feeling strong. Resolve is low. You have no stamina. There's a lack of toughness. Someone can't be counted on. The power to prevail is low.

Early Phase: You may begin to feel stronger. Energy may return. You may become more determined. The will to survive may grow. Your power may build.

Late Phase: Your strength is declining. You're no longer feeling vigorous. You've lost heart. Energy is draining out of the situation. People are losing resolve. The peak of power is past.

Keyword: Patience

Absent: There's little patience at the moment. You can't keep your temper. There's little self-control. You're having trouble waiting. No one is accepting. Frustration throws you off.

Early Phase: You may become more patient. It may get easier to wait. You may develop calm endurance. You may need to bide your time. People may become more accepting.

Late Phase: You're losing patience. You can't wait any longer. The period of resigned acceptance is over. Suffering in silence is no longer an option. You're losing your composure.

Keyword: Compassion

Absent: There's a lack of compassion. You don't feel sympathetic. Someone is not being kind. Mistakes are not being tolerated. Tender feelings can't be expressed. Pity is lacking.

Early Phase: You may start to feel sympathy. Tolerance may grow. People may show more kindness. A mood of good will may develop. You may begin to feel sorry for someone.

Late Phase: Compassion is fading. You no longer feel kindly disposed. The era of good intentions is ending. Well-meaning gestures are becoming less frequent.

Keyword: Soft Control

Absent: You're not using soft control. Someone refuses to be manipulated. Persuasion is not working. You're not wearing velvet gloves. Attempts to influence are not subtle.

Early Phase: You may start to guide indirectly. You're considering a delicate approach. People may become more accommodating. A lighter touch may be applied in the future.

Late Phase: The period of benevolent control is ending. You're no longer open to influence. Attempts to persuade are decreasing. People are less willing to go along gracefully.

THE HERMIT

Upright

It's a time of introspection. You can learn much by looking within. Searching for answers is important right now. Guidance can be given and received. There's a need for solitude. Someone is withdrawing from involvement.

Reversed

Keyword: Introspection

Absent: You're not feeling introspective right now. There's little time for inner exploring. Motivations are not an issue. Unconscious material is inaccessible. You can't focus on yourself.

Early Phase: You may start to look within. You may begin to question your identity. You may have more time to think in the future. Quiet time may become important. An inner journey may be approaching.

Late Phase: Your period of soul-searching is past. You're less inclined to focus inward now. You had a significant inner experience. Self-analysis is no longer necessary.

Keyword: Searching

Absent: You're not seeking right now. A personal quest is on hold. Someone is not looking for the truth. The hunt is stalled. No one is pursuing the investigation.

Early Phase: You may begin to look for answers. You may need to learn more. People may initiate a search. A quest may begin. Someone may start looking below the surface.

Late Phase: The search is ending. You're no longer curious to learn more. A period of questioning is behind you. The hunger for truth is fading. The desire to look around is decreasing.

Keyword: Guidance

Absent: There's little guidance. You're not offering or receiving advice. Someone's opinion is not welcome. A mentor or teacher is unavailable. Wisdom is hard to come by.

Early Phase: You may decide to seek guidance. An outside opinion may become useful. An encounter with a teacher or guru may occur in the future. You may begin a therapeutic program.

Late Phase: You're losing a source of guidance. Your counsel is no longer desired. There's less help available now. Someone is rejecting supervision. Suggestions are dwindling.

Keyword: Solitude

Absent: Solitude is not possible. You can't withdraw from the situation. You have little desire to be alone. Someone is not in seclusion now. You can't get away from it all.

Early Phase: You may become more private. A need for solitude may grow. Someone may decide to live alone. You may be more isolated in the future. Quiet time may gain appeal.

Late Phase: Your period of solitude is ending. You're no longer on your own. The feelings of separation are fading. There's less need to be apart now. Someone is leaving a private world.

WHEEL OF FORTUNE

Upright

It's a time of destiny. Your fate is greeting you. A turning point has been reached. Which way will you go? There is great movement and change. A person vision is meaningful to you and others.

Reversed

Keyword: Destiny

Absent: You're denying your destiny. You're not taking advantage of chance. It's hard to accept this special moment. Your fate is not in your hands. Karma is not being resolved.

Early Phase: You may begin to sense the action of fate. A chance encounter may become important. The threads of your life may come together. A surprise twist may be possible in the future.

Late Phase: The moment of destiny has passed. You're no longer open to the fortunes of fate. An unexpected event is behind you. The role of chance is decreasing. The karmic moment has played itself out.

Keyword: Turning Point

Absent: You're not accepting a turning point. You don't want to look at change. Someone is resisting a new possibility. Reversals are not an option. A change in course is stalled for the moment.

Early Phase: A turning point may be coming up. You're considering a change of direction. A surprising turn of events could occur. The situation may reverse itself in the future.

Late Phase: The turning point is behind you. Change is less likely at this point. You're no longer open to a new direction. Options are narrowing. A course has been set, one way or the other.

Keyword: Movement

Absent: There's little movement now. The activity level is low. You're not getting involved. There's not much happening. New developments are rare. The pace is slow.

Early Phase: The pace may pick up. You may start to notice more activity. People may move around more. The agitation may become more obvious. Everyone may begin to hurry.

Late Phase: There's less activity now. The pace is slowing. You're no longer moving around much. The number of changes is decreasing. There's less switching around.

Keyword: Personal Vision

Absent: You're lacking a personal vision. You're not sure of your role and purpose. You've lost touch with your goals. Nothing seems to make sense. The connections don't add up.

Early Phase: You may become more aware. You may begin to understand yourself. Patterns may start to make sense. Your outlook may expand. An epiphany may occur in the future.

Late Phase: Your personal vision is behind you. You're moving beyond a moment of clarity. Your perspective is no longer all-encompassing. There's less understanding now. You're losing touch with your dream.

JUSTICE

Upright

It's a time of justice. Matters of principle and fair play are important. Responsibility is an issue. People are being held accountable. A decision is being reached. The action of cause and effect is clear.

Reversed

Keyword: Justice

Absent: There's little justice. The fair solution is not on the table. You're not being impartial. People are not committed to what's right. Someone's not getting a fair deal. Legal matters are not being resolved.

Early Phase: You're thinking of seeking justice. Questions of fairness may come up. Principles may become important. Someone may seek equal treatment. You may get involved with the law.

Late Phase: The time for justice has passed. You're no longer concerned with a legal matter. The focus on equality is decreasing. Principles are being abandoned. Fair play is less of an issue now.

Keyword: Responsibility

Absent: No one is taking responsibility. Someone is not being accountable. You're not willing to take the heat. Old debts are going unsettled. The obligation is not yours. No one is to blame.

Early Phase: You may start to assume responsibility. You're thinking of taking charge. Someone may admit involvement. People may become more reliable. You may need to answer for your deeds.

Late Phase: The conscientious period is ending. People are less willing to meet obligations. You no longer have to bear the brunt. The finger-pointing is behind you. Someone is not as trustworthy now.

Keyword: Decision

Absent: A decision is not being made. A judgment has not been rendered. No one is coming to a conclusion. The jury is out. You can't make up your mind. Someone is avoiding a choice.

Early Phase: You may be approaching a decision. A need for resolution may develop. You may start to explore options. Someone may need to weigh all sides. The verdict may be on the way.

Late Phase: The period of judgment is past. A choice has been made, or the time for choosing is ending. A verdict was rendered. Someone is less decisive now. Resolution is no longer important.

Keyword: Cause and Effect

Absent: You can't see a cause and effect relationship. Reasons aren't clear to you. You don't understanding the connections. The karma of the situation is obscure. Results don't match efforts.

Early Phase: You may begin to see patterns. The impact of the past may become obvious. The situation may start to make sense. You may be causing future effects now.

Late Phase: The cause and effect connections are less clear. You no longer understand why. A fateful result has occurred, and you don't recognize the cause.

THE HANGED MAN

Upright

It's a time of letting go. You can surrender to your experience. A reversal is possible. The situation may change completely. A feeling of suspension exists. Action and time are on hold. A sacrifice is in the air.

Reversed

Keyword: Letting Go

Absent: You're having trouble letting go. Emotions are not being released. Someone is resisting. The struggle is not over. You can't accept what is.

Early Phase: You may begin to relinquish control. You may become more vulnerable. You may need to surrender in the future. Someone may be getting ready to yield. You may have to renounce a claim.

Late Phase: The time for letting go is over. The release is behind you now. Someone or something was set free. The mood is less open now. The moment for capitulation has passed.

Keyword: Reversal

Absent: A reversal is not happening. You're not changing your mind. The old order is not being replaced. Someone is not doing an about-face. You're not switching to the opposite.

Early Phase: A change of direction may be approaching. You may be thinking of switching. Someone may be going to flip. You may need to turn the situation around. A ruling may be overturned.

Late Phase: The moment for reversal is behind you. The situation is less likely to change now. You're no longer thinking of switching. The urge to revoke or recant is decreasing.

Keyword: Suspension

Absent: Actions are not being held up. You're not being left hanging. There's little pause in activity. People are not waiting for the best moment. No one is suspended. You're not living in the moment.

Early Phase: You may begin to feel cut off. An interruption may be approaching. An event may be put on hold. The chance of delay may grow. Activity may cease in the future.

Late Phase: The period of suspension is past. You're no longer on hold. The feeling of timelessness is fading. There's less chance for a pause now. The break is ending.

Keyword: Sacrifice

Absent: No sacrifice is occurring. You're not giving up a claim. Someone is not being a martyr. A concession is not being offered. Something is not being relinquished.

Early Phase: You're thinking of making a sacrifice. You're considering putting someone else's needs first. You may start to devote yourself to a cause. The need to do without may increase.

Late Phase: A time of sacrifice is behind you. You no longer need to deny yourself. There's less call for selfless service now. The need to do without is decreasing. The mood of martyrdom is fading.

DEATH

Upright

It's a time of ending. Something is finishing. A transition is in progress. You're moving from one state to another. Elimination is important. It's possible to get rid of excess. Inexorable forces are having a strong impact.

Reversed

Keyword: Ending

Absent: An ending is not occurring. You're not completing a task. Goodbyes are not being said. A door is not closing. The last act is not over. Nothing is final yet.

Early Phase: You may be approaching an ending. A parting of the ways may be coming up. You may be entering the end game. A task may be nearing completion. Someone may decide to call it a day.

Late Phase: The time of ending is past. The completion is behind you. Unfinished business is no longer an issue. The old ways are fading. The urge to terminate is decreasing.

Keyword: Transition

Absent: A transition is not in progress. You're not changing status. A transformation is not occurring. A shift is not taking place. You're not being cast adrift.

Early Phase: You may enter a period of transition. A change of condition may be on the horizon. The tide may begin to shift. Someone may be nearing an in-between state. A major transformation may become possible.

Late Phase: A transition is behind you. You're no longer moving from one state to another. A passage is almost completed. People are less interested in change now. The need for conversion is decreasing.

Keyword: Elimination

Absent: Nothing is being eliminated. You're not getting rid of excess. No one is being cast out. A removal is not happening. You can't focus on basics. Unwanted attitudes are not being purged.

Early Phase: You may start to get rid of baggage. Something may be jettisoned in the future. Nonessentials may be on the way out. A dismissal may be in the works. You may begin to simplify.

Late Phase: The period of elimination is behind you. A paring down is less likely now. You're no longer concerned about a removal. The cut has been made. The need to do away with is fading.

Keyword: Inexorable Forces

Absent: The situation is not set in stone. Your fate is not sealed. You don't have to give up. Sweeping changes are not in effect. Dramatic results are not happening. The power of the moment is blocked.

Early Phase: An irresistible event may be on the horizon. An earth-shaking experience may be coming up. Powerful happenings may be building strength. You may get drawn into an inescapable scenario.

Late Phase: A powerful moment is behind you. You've gone through a fateful encounter. A larger-than-life experience has passed. You're no longer at the mercy of forces. The situation is less unyielding now.

TEMPERANCE

Upright

It's a time of temperance and moderation. The middle ground holds opportunity. Balance is important. All factors are in equilibrium. Good health is evident. Finding the right combination is possible.

Reversed

Keyword: Temperance

Absent: There's a lack of temperance. You're not being moderate. Someone is not maintaining self-control. You're having trouble showing restraint. Sobriety is not being embraced.

Early Phase: You may start to be more moderate. You're thinking of abstaining. Someone may look for the middle ground. A centrist position may gain momentum. Forbearance may increase.

Late Phase: The period of moderation is ending. There's less restraint now. You're no longer feeling temperate. The urge to be low-key is fading. Discretion is disappearing.

Keyword: Balance

Absent: There's a lack of balance. All positions are not equal. Parity is not being maintained. Parts aren't symmetrical. Harmony is missing. You're not feeling calm and steady. Your composure is shaken.

Early Phase: The situation may grow more balanced. Equilibrium may become a goal. You may start to feel more composed. A focus on equality may begin. You may keep your cool in the future.

Late Phase: The period of balance is ending. Sides are no longer equal. There's less harmony now. A stable situation is breaking up. You're losing composure.

Keyword: Health

Absent: Good health is lacking. Your physical condition is poor. Energy is low. Someone does not feel vigorous and strong. You lack a sense of well-being. Recovery is slow.

Early Phase: Vitality may return. A recovery may begin. You may start to concentrate on your health. More energy may become available. Physical conditioning may improve.

Late Phase: Health is declining. You're feeling less vigorous. The energetic phase is ending. Someone is no longer well. The period of comfort and ease is passing.

Keyword: Combination

Absent: Forces are not being combined. People are not joining together. You're not pooling your resources. The right mix is not in place. Synthesis is lacking.

Early Phase: A merger may occur in the future. A union may become possible. You may start to blend in. An alliance may form. Elements may come together.

Late Phase: An association is breaking up. Parties are no longer joined. There's less consolidation now. The mixture is dissolving. Bonds are not as strong.

THE DEVIL

Upright

It's a time of bondage and obsession. The pull of materialism is strong. Ignorance of the truth is causing concern. Facts are hidden or obscured. There is a mood of hopelessness. The future seems dark and uncertain.

Reversed

Keyword: Bondage

Absent: You're not tied down. An addiction is not controlling. Someone is not willing to submit. You're resisting an obsession. There is no loss of freedom. You're denying a compulsion.

Early Phase: You may begin to feel controlled. An obsession may form. Someone may get hooked. The walls may start to close in. You may be heading into a limiting situation.

Late Phase: The period of bondage is ending. You're putting an obsession behind you. An addiction is less powerful now. You no longer need to submit. A fixation is decreasing.

Keyword: Materialism

Absent: There's a lack of materialism. You're not focused on the physical. The urge to spend is being resisted. Someone is not interested in possessions. Luxury is not important.

Early Phase: You may begin to focus on the material. Acquiring may become important. A desire for physical pleasure may grow. You may start to wish for more comfortable surroundings.

Late Phase: You're losing interest in material possessions. Your desire to spend is decreasing. Surface appearances are less important now. You're no longer focused on the senses.

Keyword: Ignorance

Absent: Ignorance is not a problem. You're not in the dark. Appearances are not deceiving. Being oblivious is not an option. Someone is not blind to the truth.

Early Phase: You may become uninformed. The truth may start to be obscured. You may get out of touch. Someone may begin to look the other way.

Late Phase: The time of not knowing is over. You're no longer ignorant of the truth. Being unenlightened is less desirable now. Your lack of awareness is ending.

Keyword: Hopelessness

Absent: There's no lack of faith. You're not despairing. No one is giving up. You're resisting negativity. The worst scenario is not acceptable. All is not lost.

Early Phase: You may begin to lose hope. Doubts may grow. The future may seem less promising. Your faith may be challenged. A mood of pessimism may develop.

Late Phase: A hopeless period is behind you. Feelings of despair are fading. The world seems less hostile now. You're no longer consumed by doubt. The atmosphere of gloom is lifting.

THE TOWER

Upright

It's a time of sudden change. Plans are being disrupted. There's a strong release of emotion and energy. A downfall is in progress. Someone's fortunes are being upset. A revelation is occurring. All is being exposed.

Reversed

Keyword: Sudden Change

Absent: Sudden changes are not happening. There's no crisis at the moment. Routines are not being disrupted. You're resisting chaos. There are no surprises.

Early Phase: A crisis may be developing. A major shakeup may be coming. A revolution may be in the works. You may experience a disruption. A drastic change may occur in the future.

Late Phase: The crisis is behind you. The period of upheaval is ending. You're no longer caught in chaos. There's less chance of a surprise now. The disruption is diminishing.

Keyword: Release

Absent: A release is not occurring. You're not letting your feelings out. An explosion is being contained. Energy is not getting discharged. An emotional outburst is not happening.

Early Phase: Anger may be building. You're getting ready to explode. You may need to let it all out. The dam may break in the future. A release of energy may become necessary.

Late Phase: The release is behind you. An emotional explosion occurred. You no longer want to lash out. Loss of control is less likely now. The anger is decreasing.

Keyword: Downfall

Absent: A downfall is not occurring. A crash is not in effect. Fortunes aren't lost. Someone is not being humbled. You're resisting a blow to the ego.

Early Phase: A downfall may be in the works. A humbling experience may occur in the future. Someone may topple from the heights. You may be heading toward a collapse.

Late Phase: The downfall is behind you. A period of ruin is over. The breakdown is in the past. You're no longer concerned about failing. The plunge has already occurred.

Keyword: Revelation

Absent: There's no revelation. You don't realize the whole truth. The flash of insight is not occurring. Someone is not seeing past illusions. Answers are not forthcoming.

Early Phase: You may be heading toward a revelation. The truth may be revealed. You may be able to see everything in a flash. An eye-opener may be on the horizon.

Late Phase: A surprise disclosure has occurred. The truth has been divulged. You experienced a burst of awareness. A revelation is behind you. Someone is no longer exposing the truth.

THE STAR

Upright

It's a time of hope and faith. The situation is full of promise. Inspiration is in the air. Creative answers are possible. A spirit of generosity is important. Giving freely makes a difference. Serenity is possible within and without.

Reversed

Keyword: Hope

Absent: There's a lack of hope. You don't believe in the future. Someone is not thinking positively. Faith is not strong. You can't see the silver lining.

Early Phase: Hope may grow. You may start to feel more confident in the future. The chance for success may improve. Expectations may rise.

Late Phase: Hope is fading. You no longer have faith in a positive outcome. The light at the end of the tunnel is disappearing. Belief is not as strong now. Your spirits are sinking.

Keyword: Inspiration

Absent: Inspiration is missing. You're not getting the answer. Motivation is not strong. A flash of insight is eluding you. Creativity is stalled. You lack someone to encourage you.

Early Phase: You may begin to get inspired. The creative impulse may grow. Someone may become motivated. A positive example may spur you on. You may be stimulated to a higher level.

Late Phase: The period of inspiration is fading. You're less motivated now. The way is no longer clear. The call to greatness is fading. Encouragement is harder to come by.

Keyword: Generosity

Absent: You're not giving gladly. Your heart is not open. Love cannot flow freely. Someone can't extend an offer. A gift is not free of strings. Wealth is not being shared.

Early Phase: You may start to feel generous. A gift may be on the horizon. A spirit of sharing may develop. Someone may extend love and forgiveness. You may contribute openly in the future.

Late Phase: A time of generosity is ending. You're no longer willing or able to offer support. Your heart is not as open now. The charitable impulse is fading. There's less desire to spare no expense.

Keyword: Serenity

Absent: Serenity is lacking. You don't have peace of mind. The situation is not harmonious. It's not easy to relax. You can't maintain your cool.

Early Phase: The environment may become peaceful. You may start to feel calmer. Tranquility may be restored. A period of serenity may be approaching.

Late Phase: You're no longer feeling calm. The mood of serenity is fading. You're losing your ability to stay centered. People are less in harmony now. The moment of peace is behind you.

THE MOON

Upright

It's a time of fear and uncertainty. Feelings of anxiety are strong. Someone is caught in an illusion. A fantasy seems real. The world of imagination is key. Events are strange and unusual. Bewilderment is a problem.

Reversed

Keyword: Fear

Absent: You're not afraid right now. A phobia is not strong. Someone is resisting a fear. Feelings of dread are not obvious. The shadow self cannot surface.

Early Phase: You may start to feel anxious. A mood of uncertainty may develop. Someone may become apprehensive. A hidden fear may surface. You may begin to feel some qualms.

Late Phase: Fears are diminishing. An inner demon is less powerful now. You're no longer intimidated. The anxious moments are behind you. The mood of foreboding is disappearing.

Keyword: Illusion

Absent: There's no illusion. You're not under a false impression. The truth is not being distorted. People aren't deceiving themselves. An attempt to mislead is not working. You're not chasing a fantasy.

Early Phase: You may get drawn into an illusion. A false picture may develop. You may start to deceive yourself. The truth may become elusive. Hallucinations may get stronger.

Late Phase: An illusion has been revealed. Appearances are no longer deceiving. The false reality is losing its hold. You're less susceptible to fantasy. Someone has stopped trying to fool you.

Keyword: Imagination

Absent: There's a lack of imagination. People aren't open to the unusual. You can't remember your dreams. Visions are elusive. The unconscious is not available. You're not prone to fantasy right now.

Early Phase: You may begin to use your imagination. You may open to what is strange and bizarre. Unconscious material may surface. Someone may start to indulge in make-believe.

Late Phase: A fantasy is no longer strong. You're less imaginative now. Someone is losing interest in dreams. Fanciful notions are decreasing. The strange happenings are decreasing.

Keyword: Bewilderment

Absent: You're not feeling confused. You haven't lost direction and purpose. Someone is not easily distracted. Circumstances are not puzzling. You have no trouble thinking clearly.

Early Phase: You may start to get disoriented. Uncertainty may grow. The way may become unclear. Someone may begin to get lost. You may lose your bearings.

Late Phase: The period of bewilderment is behind you. You're no longer confused. The aimless wandering is over. The mental fog is lifting. Someone is less disoriented now.

THE SUN

Upright

It's a time of enlightenment. New levels of understanding are being realized. Greatness is yours. You are shining forth brilliantly. Health and vitality are strong. You have the assurance you need for success.

Reversed

Keyword: Enlightenment

Absent: You're not realizing the truth. You're not feeling enlightened. There's a lack of understanding. You can't make sense of the situation. The pieces don't fit together.

Early Phase: You may begin to understand. Insights may start to come. You may get closer to a breakthrough. Someone may have an epiphany. An expanded vision may become possible.

Late Phase: The moment of enlightenment is behind you. You experienced an epiphany. There's less awareness now. You're losing your grasp of the truth. The sun is going behind a cloud.

Keyword: Greatness

Absent: Greatness is elusive. You can't achieve your goal. A moment of glory is not happening. Someone is not the center of attention. No one is outstanding right now.

Early Phase: You may start to be noticed. Your light may get brighter. Your talent may develop. A glorious moment may be approaching. Someone may show great promise.

Late Phase: A period of renown is ending. You're no longer standing out. The height of success is behind you. Fame is slipping away. Your time as leader is winding down.

Keyword: Vitality

Absent: There's a lack of vitality. Your strength is low. A vital spark is missing. Someone is not vigorous. You don't feel zest for life. The atmosphere is not energized.

Early Phase: You may begin to feel animated. The mood may pick up. Your vigor may return. Enthusiasm may grow. People may start to get charged.

Late Phase: Your vitality is decreasing. You no longer have much energy. The life force is diminishing. The dynamic period is behind you. There's less zip in your step now.

Keyword: Assurance

Absent: You're not feeling confident. Assurance is low. Someone can't make a guarantee. There's a lack of certainty. You're afraid to show what you can do.

Early Phase: You may gain some assurance. You may start to trust your abilities. Confidence may return. You may become free and expansive.

Late Phase: You're less confident now. You're no longer certain. People are losing their nerve. Your faith in yourself is fading. Convictions are not as strong now.

JUDGEMENT

Upright

It's a time of judgment. A tough decision is being weighed. A moment of rebirth is at hand. A fresh start is happening. You sense an inner calling. You know what you must do. Absolution is possible. Forgiveness is in the air.

Reversed

Keyword: Judgment

Absent: You can't pass judgment. You're not being judged. A decision is not being made. A ruling is not available. No one is making an assessment. Someone is not able to take a stand.

Early Phase: You may have to judge. You're preparing to make a choice. An opinion may be rendered. Someone may get off the fence. A conclusion may be reached.

Late Phase: There's less judging now. Your actions are no longer under scrutiny. A decision has been made. A day of reckoning is behind you. The period of criticism is ending.

Keyword: Rebirth

Absent: You're not feeling reborn. A transformation is not happening. Someone is not opening to possibilities. A fresh start is failing. Hope is not being renewed.

Early Phase: Someone may start over. A renewal may be in progress. A time of awakening may be coming. You may see everything differently in the future.

Late Phase: The fresh start is ending. A transforming experience is behind you. The bright new beginning is past. Your new-found hope is fading. You're less joyful now.

Keyword: Inner Calling

Absent: You're not aware of your calling. You can't decide on a vocation. You're not sure what you want to do. There's a lack of conviction. Someone is afraid to make a difference.

Early Phase: You may begin to see your path. You may become drawn in a new direction. Self-confidence may be growing. The way forward may get clearer.

Late Phase: You're losing your sense of purpose. You no longer feel committed to a chosen field. Your certainty is draining away. Someone has failed to heed a call.

Keyword: Absolution

Absent: You're not being absolved of guilt. Someone is unable to atone. You're reluctant to ask for forgiveness. You can't release your regrets. Your remorse is not believed.

Early Phase: You may start to seek forgiveness. You may begin to unburden yourself. It may become possible to wipe the slate clean. Someone may be getting ready to atone.

Late Phase: You experienced absolution. Your guilt has been washed away. The desire to atone is fading. A reprieve is less likely now. Someone is no longer willing to overlook an offense.

THE WORLD

Upright

It's a time of integration. All aspects are coming together. Your accomplishment is being recognized. Dreams are coming true. Involvement is important. You feel fully engaged. There's a sense of fulfillment.

Reversed

Keyword: Integration

Absent: There's a lack of integration. People are not joining together. No one is working in unison. You're not feeling whole. There's no connection. Dynamic balance is missing.

Early Phase: You may begin to feel whole. Everything may start coming together. A spirit of unity may develop. A synthesis may become possible. You may be approaching a time of togetherness.

Late Phase: A combination is coming apart. People are no longer united. You're losing your sense of completeness. The parts are separating. There's less coordination now.

Keyword: Accomplishment

Absent: Little is being accomplished. You can't realize your goals. The path to achievement is blocked. There's a lack of productivity. A dream is not manifesting. Prosperity is elusive.

Early Phase: You may be moving toward your goals. Achievements may become possible. A dream may start to be realized. You may start taking your first steps toward success. Prosperity may be returning.

Late Phase: An accomplishment is behind you. A period of achievement is over. You're no longer meeting your goals. The chance to realize your dream is fading. The era of prosperity is ending.

Keyword: Involvement

Absent: There's a lack of involvement. Few people are taking part. You're not feeling engaged. The buy-in is not strong. A gift or talent is not being used. Someone is not wholly committed.

Early Phase: You may begin to get involved. Someone may join the effort. You're getting ready to contribute. A desire to serve may grow. Connections may be forged in the future.

Late Phase: There's less involvement now. You're no longer feeling engaged. Someone is pulling away. A period of intense activity is ending. The focus on serving is decreasing.

Keyword: Fulfillment

Absent: You're not feeling fulfilled. There's a lack of contentment. You can't savor the present. Someone is dissatisfied. The moment is not complete. You can't enjoy life. Joy is rare.

Early Phase: You may become more contented. Moments of happiness may start to happen. A feeling of satisfaction may grow. A time of fulfillment may be approaching.

Late Phase: There's less satisfaction now. You're not as content as you were. The mood of happiness is fading. You no longer have peace of mind.

MINOR ARCANA

ACE OF WANDS

Upright

Wands' fire energy is at your disposal right now. There's an opportunity to use creative force. You can expand your experience of enthusiasm, confidence, and courage.

Reversed

Keyword: Creative Force

Absent: The opportunity to use creative force is missing. You lack an outlet for your abilities. Your talents can't unfold. Nothing new is being proposed. No one is offering a different approach.

Early Phase: You may have a chance to be creative. An original idea may materialize. Someone may come up with a novel approach. A venue for your talent could open up.

Late Phase: The opportunity to use creative force is fading. The chance to do something new is past. The support for original ideas is disappearing. Creative moments are less frequent.

Keyword: Enthusiasm

Absent: The opportunity to be enthusiastic is missing. No one wants to make an effort. You can't contribute actively. The desire is not there. People can't generate any excitement.

Early Phase: You may have a chance to be enthusiastic. An inspiring occasion may occur. Someone may present an exciting proposal. You may back a winner. Support may start building.

Late Phase: The opportunity to be enthusiastic is fading. You're less eager to take part. The ride seems to be over. You're no longer up for the challenge. There are fewer reasons to be optimistic now.

Keyword: Confidence

Absent: The opportunity to show confidence is missing. You can't prove what you can do. No one believes in you. The environment isn't encouraging. You're having trouble convincing others.

Early Phase: You may have a chance to show confidence. An opportunity to prove yourself may be on the way. A test of your skills may be coming up. Your belief in yourself may be put on the line.

Late Phase: The opportunity to show confidence is fading. The moment to convince someone has passed. You can't demonstrate your certainty now. People are no longer focused on your performance.

Keyword: Courage

Absent: The opportunity to show courage is missing. Your bravery is not being tested. You can't face your fear. There are no challenges right now. You can't push past your limits.

Early Phase: You may have a chance to show courage. You may have to face a challenge. A time of testing may be approaching. You may be asked to take a stand.

Late Phase: The opportunity to show courage is fading. You're no longer being challenged. The test of your mettle is past. The fearful situation is ending.

TWO OF WANDS

Upright

It's a time of personal power. You have influence and authority. Others are following your lead. Boldness is the order of the day. It's possible to take risks. Someone's approach shows originality.

Reversed

Keyword: Personal Power

Absent: You lack personal power at the moment. You have little influence. Others are not accepting your authority. You're not asking for the respect that is due. You can't call the shots right now.

Early Phase: You may gain more power. Others may start paying attention to you. Your position may get stronger. You may be able to seize control. You may be put in charge in the future.

Late Phase: Your power is fading. It's no longer as easy to assert authority. People are not paying as much attention to you. The reins are slipping out of your hands.

Keyword: Boldness

Absent: You're not being bold. It's not possible to confront the situation head-on. Someone is failing to take the initiative. No one is speaking out. You're not comfortable gambling or taking risks.

Early Phase: You may become bold. You may need to take a risk. Daring gestures may become necessary. You may have to seize the initiative. A chance to make your move may open up.

Late Phase: You're feeling less daring. Your courage is slipping. The chance to take a risk has passed. You're pulling back from a dangerous situation. The urge to gamble is fading.

Keyword: Originality

Absent: There's a lack of originality. Nothing new is going on. You don't have a chance to do your own thing. No one is taking a novel approach. People are not ready to accept a pioneer.

Early Phase: You may become more creative. It may get easier to diverge from the crowd. A novel path may open up. You may have a unique experience. Something new may occur.

Late Phase: You're feeling less creative. There are fewer novel approaches now. It's no longer easy to adopt your own style. You had a unique experience that is now ending.

THREE OF WANDS

Upright

It's a time of exploration. You're seeking adventures and new experiences. Foresight is important. It's possible to plan for the future. Questions of leadership are a factor. Someone can provide needed direction.

Reversed

Keyword: Exploration

Absent: There's little exploring going on. People are not open to adventure. You'd rather not deal with unknowns right now. No one is pushing the envelope at the moment.

Early Phase: You're thinking of exploring new possibilities. An adventure may begin. The future may be more open. You may move into unfamiliar territory. Someone may decide to test uncharted waters.

Late Phase: A period of adventure is ending. The desire to explore is fading. You're no longer interested in dealing with unknowns. There's less need to seek novelty now.

Keyword: Foresight

Absent: There's a lack of foresight. No one is looking at the long-term implications. Grand visions are not being well received. People are not paying attention to the future.

Early Phase: You may need to plan for the future. People may begin taking the long view. It may be possible to foresee problems. You may get premonitions of what's to come.

Late Phase: Attempts to plan for the future are fading. You're no longer showing foresight. There's less focus on looking ahead. People are less interested in the big picture.

Keyword: Leadership

Absent: There's no leadership. Someone has stopped providing direction. You're not in a position to assume control. You can't get a group's support. You're reluctant to show the way.

Early Phase: You may be moving into a leadership position. A chance to take command may open up. You may need to set an example. The main role may fall to you. You may be chosen as a representative.

Late Phase: The opportunity to take command is fading. Your leadership role is behind you. You're no longer setting an example. There's less direction than before. A commander is stepping down.

FOUR OF WANDS

Upright

It's a time of celebration. People are rejoicing over a happy event or success. You're recognizing a milestone. Freedom is important. It's possible to break free of limitations. Excitement is in the air.

Reversed

Keyword: Celebration

Absent: There's little celebration going on. The ceremony is not going forward. The party is off. Achievements are not being recognized. No one is prepared to claim success.

Early Phase: A major celebration may be approaching. You may experience a joyous occasion. A milestone may be reached. You may receive some congratulations.

Late Phase: The event or ceremony is behind you. The festivities are ending. A milestone was reached and passed. The mood of rejoicing is fading. You no longer have much reason to celebrate.

Keyword: Freedom

Absent: There's a lack of freedom right now. You can't loose the ties that bind. The time's not right for escape. Someone can't accept your independence. No one is being released.

Early Phase: You may decide to claim your freedom. You may let go of inhibitions. You may need to plan an escape. You may cut some cords. Delivery may be at hand.

Late Phase: The break for freedom is behind you. You made your escape. The cords have been cut. You no longer need to assert your independence. A period of unlimited possibility is ending.

Keyword: Excitement

Absent: There's little excitement. Not much is going on. Adventure is not a high priority at the moment. People lack enthusiasm. No surprises are happening.

Early Phase: You may start looking for excitement. You may begin seeking thrills. A big adventure may be approaching. Enthusiasm may grow. A surprise may occur.

Late Phase: The mood of excitement is fading. You're not as enthusiastic as you were. Thrills are not as important now. The spirit of adventure is not as strong. The commotion is dying down.

FIVE OF WANDS

Upright

It's a time of disagreement and petty quarrels. Everyone is at cross-purposes. Competition is a factor. You have a rival or opponent. Hassles are a problem. You are experiencing minor setbacks.

Reversed

Keyword: Disagreement

Absent: There's little disagreement. Quarrels are nonexistent. People are not picking fights. Debate is being squelched. You're not allowed to question the situation.

Early Phase: You may begin to disagree. Arguments may break out. The lack of consensus may become obvious. People could start quibbling over details.

Late Phase: Disagreements are decreasing. People are no longer arguing much. The period of contention is ending. Differences are not as obvious now. The debate is coming to a close.

Keyword: Competition

Absent: There's little competition. No one's challenging you at the moment. The contest is not in progress. People are not pitted against each other. The match or tournament is not happening.

Early Phase: Competitive elements may increase. A rivalry may develop. You may have a run-in with an opponent. A match may be coming up. A challenge may occur in the future.

Late Phase: The competition is ending. There's less opposition now. You no longer have to deal with a rival or challenger. The match is behind you. People are not as concerned with outdoing each other.

Keyword: Hassles

Absent: You're not experiencing hassles. Petty distractions are not a problem. You're not concerned with trivial details. No roadblocks are in sight.

Early Phase: You may experience a few setbacks. Minor irritations may increase. Some hassles may develop in the future. You may have to deal with some annoying problems.

Late Phase: The hassles are decreasing. You've worked through the worst problems. Resistance is no longer slowing you down. The demands are not as bothersome now.

SIX OF WANDS

Upright

It's a time of triumph and success. Victory is in the air. You are enjoying acclaim and well-deserved recognition. Pride is an issue. Self-esteem is turning into arrogance.

Reversed

Keyword: Triumph

Absent: Victory is not happening. Success is not forthcoming. You're not winning right now. Someone is not prevailing. There's little vindication.

Early Phase: You may see signs of success. Victory may be getting closer. Your day of vindication may be approaching. Someone may start winning.

Late Phase: The victory is behind you. The time for success has passed. People are losing their concern with the contest. Chances for vindication are decreasing. You're no longer focused on winning.

Keyword: Acclaim

Absent: Your work is not being acknowledged. There's no applause right now. The award or prize is not being offered. You can't seem to get noticed. Someone is out of the limelight.

Early Phase: You may receive an award or acknowledgement. Hard work may begin to pay off. Your efforts may be recognized. Fame may become important. People may start taking notice.

Late Phase: Praise and acclaim are fading. Your efforts are no longer being recognized. The prize or reward is behind you. Someone received a compliment or pat on the back.

Keyword: Pride

Absent: There's little pride now. People are not confident. Self-esteem is low. Someone is hiding arrogance. You don't have a high opinion of yourself.

Early Phase: You may become more confident. Arrogance may become a problem. Someone may be condescending. Healthy pride may change to over-confidence.

Late Phase: Your pride has taken a blow. You went through a humbling experience. You're feeling less confident. There's less arrogance now. People are no longer sure of themselves.

SEVEN OF WANDS

Upright

It's a time of aggression. The advantage is yours if you act forcefully. Defiance is in the air. Someone is refusing to yield. There's a mood of conviction. You are standing up for what you believe.

Reversed

Keyword: Aggression

Absent: There are no hostilities right now. No one is acting aggressively. The time is not right to take what you want. You can't assert yourself. People are not going on the offensive.

Early Phase: Aggression may increase. Hostilities may break out. You may be thinking of a fight. A chance to seize the advantage may come up. You may need to make your point forcefully.

Late Phase: The period of aggression is ending. You're no longer involved in a fight. There's less chance to state your case now. The advantage is no longer yours. Someone has already fired the first shot.

Keyword: Defiance

Absent: Resistance seems futile. No one is being defiant. You can't defend yourself at the moment. It's not possible to hold your position. The time is not right to make a challenge.

Early Phase: You may become more defiant. Resistance may increase. You may need to defend your position. Someone could decide to hold out. People may get their back up.

Late Phase: You're no longer resisting. Defiance is decreasing. Opposition is not as strong now. Challengers are backing off. Refusals are no longer a problem.

Keyword: Conviction

Absent: There's a lack of conviction. No one is sure. It's not easy to stay firm. Someone is not showing much character. You're not convinced you're right.

Early Phase: Conviction may grow. You may gain confidence. You may decide to stay the course. Someone may speak out forcefully. Character may become important.

Late Phase: You're becoming less certain. You're no longer convinced you're right. Someone is giving up. Firm resolutions are getting broken. People are losing the courage to speak out.

EIGHT OF WANDS

Upright

It's a time of quick action. Events are happening rapidly. You can make your move. A conclusion is in progress. Everything is coming together. News is making a difference. The truth is coming out.

Reversed

Keyword: Quick Action

Absent: Little is happening. It's not time for action. Everyone is in low gear. Plans are not being carried out. No one is making a move. Changes are not welcome.

Early Phase: You're thinking of declaring yourself openly. The pace may pick up. People may decide to act. Changes may become obvious. The time to strike may be coming. Events may start taking off.

Late Phase: The rapid changes are behind you. The pace is slowing. The time for action is past. You no longer have to rush around. You're dealing with the aftermath now.

Keyword: Conclusion

Absent: There's no end in sight. The situation is not getting resolved. No one is taking care of unfinished business. The elements are not coming together. You can't finish. It's difficult to stop.

Early Phase: You're thinking of concluding matters. The last act may begin. A final resolution may be approaching. You may be heading toward a culmination.

Late Phase: The situation has been resolved. Everything has been completed. The final act is ending. You're closing out some activity. The last word has nearly been spoken.

Keyword: News

Absent: There's no news at the moment. You lack the information you need. You can't learn more right now. The truth is not coming out. Messages are not getting through.

Early Phase: Some news may be on the way. You may hear an important announcement. You may be getting closer to the truth. Someone may initiate a meaningful conversation.

Late Phase: The news has been delivered. You found out what you needed to know. The truth came out. Less news is getting through. You're no longer in the loop. You have fewer opportunities to be informed.

NINE OF WANDS

Upright

It's a time of defensiveness. You are preparing for the worst. Extra precautions are in order. Perseverance is important. You can keep going. You have the stamina you need to see the matter through.

Reversed

Keyword: Defensiveness

Absent: There's no need to be defensive now. You're not being attacked. Protections are not in place. Someone is not being careful. People are not assuming the worst.

Early Phase: You may become wary. You may need to defend yourself. Someone may start getting paranoid. The atmosphere may become guarded. Protection may be necessary.

Late Phase: You're no longer defensive. The need to be guarded is ending. There's less chance of an attack now. The mood of paranoia is decreasing. Extra precautions are no longer required.

Keyword: Perseverance

Absent: There's a lack of persistence. You're not committed to the effort. People are not staying the course. Someone is not following through. You don't want to keep trying.

Early Phase: Your resolve may grow. You may get more committed. People may show more determination. You may decide to keep going. Multiple attempts may become necessary.

Late Phase: Commitment is weakening. You're not trying as hard now. Your resolve is fading. You got knocked down and don't want to get up again. The effort no longer seems worth it.

Keyword: Stamina

Absent: You don't have much energy. Your strength is low. It's not possible to keep up the pace. You can't go on because of fatigue. There's a lack of staying power. Reserves are depleted.

Early Phase: Your strength may return. It may get easier to keep up the pace. You may develop more stamina. You may need to hold fast. A test of staying power may be coming up.

Late Phase: Your energy is decreasing. Your strength is wearing out. It's no longer possible to keep going. Your endurance is not what it was. You're letting up a bit. The test of your staying power is ending.

TEN OF WANDS

Upright

It's a time of overextending. You're trying to do too much. Someone's shouldering most of the work. Burdens are piling up. There are too many responsibilities. You have to struggle. It's an uphill fight.

Reversed

Keyword: Overextending

Absent: You're not overextended. The work load is not excessive. No overtime is required. You don't need to do extra right now. You're not responsible for someone else.

Early Phase: You may become overextended. It may get harder to say "no." The lion's share may fall to you. There may be extra work in the future. You may have to delegate.

Late Phase: Demands are decreasing. You no longer have to shoulder the responsibility. There's less overtime now. You've passed on some of the work.

Keyword: Burdens

Absent: You aren't feeling burdened. There are few duties right now. You're not being blamed. No one is holding you accountable. The load is not too heavy at the moment.

Early Phase: You may start to feel burdened. The work may increase. You may get in over your head. A taxing problem may be looming. Worries may become more oppressive. Accountability may become an issue.

Late Phase: The burdens are decreasing. The unpleasantness is behind you. You've managed to get off the treadmill. You're no longer the main one responsible. The load is lighter now.

Keyword: Struggle

Absent: You don't need to struggle. Resistance is unnecessary. The current is not flowing against you. People are not putting up a fight. The hard way is not the only way.

Early Phase: A struggle may begin. Resistance could develop. You may need to fight for every gain. The path ahead may be steep. The opposition could make your work harder.

Late Phase: The struggle is ending. There's less resistance now. You no longer need to work so hard. The path is heading downhill. The tough times are behind you.

PAGE OF WANDS

Upright

Wands' energy is available to help you move in a new direction. The call to be creative, enthusiastic, confident, and courageous is strong right now. Take this chance to go beyond your usual limits and habits!

Reversed

Keywords: Be Creative, Be Enthusiastic, Be Confident, Be Courageous

Absent: The time is NOT right, or you CAN'T follow the call to:

take a novel approach, be original, invent a new way, express yourself freely, get excited, show passion, be the first in line, jump in with both feet, be self-assured, know you can be successful, demonstrate will, be a leader, take a risk, have an adventure, overcome fear, push past doubt.

Early Phase: The time MAY BE APPROACHING when you'll have a chance to:

use your art, show what you can do, come up with a fresh solution, use imagination, get your blood flowing, be eager, feel zest for life, support wholeheartedly, believe in yourself, have faith, accept your convictions, be sure, be assertive, jump without a net, be a hero, show your nerve.

Late Phase: The time is ENDING when you had a chance to:

show your ingenuity, be resourceful, take a different path, suggest something novel, volunteer, get behind the idea, energize others, join in the action, trust yourself, be certain, set aside doubts, put your best foot forward, make a bold move, stick your neck out, blow the whistle, take the heat.

KNIGHT OF WANDS

Upright

Wands' energy is extra strong. You, someone else, or the situation may be charming, self-confident, daring, adventurous, and passionate OR superficial, cocky, foolhardy, restless, and hot-tempered.

Reversed

Keywords (Positive): Charming, Self-Confident, Daring, Adventurous, Passionate

Keywords (Negative): Superficial, Cocky, Foolhardy, Restless, Hot-Tempered

Absent: You or someone else is NOT:

being charming, generating excitement, having complete confidence, taking on the world, risking fearlessly, becoming a hero, seeking change, rising to the challenge, being passionate, taking a vocal stand OR being insensitive, going after sexual conquests, bragging too much, overestimating abilities, taking foolish risks, being a daredevil, requiring constant stimulation, moving around restlessly, being hot-tempered, acting without thinking

Early Phase: You or another person MAY:

become physically attractive, be seductive, have a can-do attitude, be self-assured, tackle what others avoid, be bold, look for adventure, make things happen, feel strong loyalties, jump in with both feet OR avoid being serious, say or do what's expedient, show-off, be brash, make rash statements, be impetuous, refuse to set down roots, avoid commitment, get hot under the collar, lash out

Late Phase: You or another person is NO LONGER:

being glamorous, overly concerned with being attractive, convinced of a talent, being self-reliant, ready and willing to volunteer, being discrete, daring to act, ready for a challenge, feeling ardent, showing desire OR being thoughtless, focused on the superficial, overly nervy, boasting, endangering self and others, being foolhardy, constantly moving on, too restless, always ready for a fight, looking for trouble

QUEEN OF WANDS

Upright

Wands' energy is present as a state of being. A mood that is attractive, wholehearted, energetic, cheerful, and self-assured is evident. You or someone else is adopting or could adopt the mood of a cheerleader, athlete, champion, group leader, jock, host/hostess, enthusiast, master of ceremonies, or star.

Reversed

Keywords: Attractive, Wholehearted, Energetic, Cheerful, Self-assured

Absent: The mood of you or someone else is NOT:

warm, outgoing, enthusiastic, wholehearted, lively, vibrant, cheerful, upbeat, poised, unflappable

Early Phase: The mood of you or someone else MAY BECOME:

sexy, attractive, dedicated, earnest, vigorous, energetic, sunny, optimistic, self-confident, assured

Late Phase: The mood of you or someone else is NO LONGER:

appealing, popular, passionate, vivacious, active, athletic, encouraging, bright, self-possessed, composed

KING OF WANDS

Upright

Wands' energy is present in an active, outgoing way. Actions that are creative, inspiring, forceful, charismatic, and bold are evident. You or someone else is acting or could act as a leader, director, commander, pioneer, trendsetter, trailblazer, pacesetter, prophet, inventor, or creator.

Reversed

Keywords: Creative, Inspiring, Forceful, Charismatic, Bold

Absent: You or someone else is NOT:

acting creatively, developing the new, instilling confidence, leading, dominating, commanding respect, attracting attention, wowing others, demonstrating courage, confronting opposition directly

Early Phase: You or someone else MAY BEGIN to:

show more originality, take an unusual approach, generate enthusiasm, set an example, act assertively, demand compliance, get noticed, become popular, take more chances, dare to be different

Late Phase: You or someone else is NO LONGER:

taking creative chances, going in new directions, showing the way, inspiring, carrying authority well, forcing the issue, acting outrageous, being talked about, ignoring what others think, grabbing the bull by the horns

ACE OF CUPS

Upright

Cups' water energy is at your disposal right now. There's an opportunity to use emotional force. You can expand your experience of intuition, intimacy, and love.

Reversed

Keyword: Emotional Force

Absent: The opportunity to use emotional force is missing. You lack an outlet for your feelings. Your heart doesn't lead. The environment doesn't encourage passion. Strong emotions are being denied.

Early Phase: You may have a chance to use emotional force. An opportunity to express your feelings may open up. Someone may respond strongly in the future. An emotional encounter is on the horizon.

Late Phase: The chance to use emotional force is fading. The chance to show your feelings is past. The time for passion is ending. You can no longer respond from the heart.

Keyword: Intuition

Absent: The opportunity to be intuitive is missing. No one respects your hunches. You can't contribute your insights. Inner awareness is not present. You're not trusting your gut reaction.

Early Phase: You may have a chance to be intuitive. Some time to go within may open up. An experience of direct knowing could occur. A psychic occasion is coming up.

Late Phase: The opportunity to be intuitive is fading. You're less able to go within now. Experiences of direct knowing are decreasing. Your gut reactions are no longer strong.

Keyword: Intimacy

Absent: The opportunity to be intimate is missing. You don't have a chance to get close to someone. You're not in a relationship right now. A bond is broken. Someone won't go to a deeper level.

Early Phase: You may have a chance to be intimate. A moment of closeness is approaching. There's a potential for sharing in the situation. A new relationship is possible in the future.

Late Phase: The opportunity to be intimate is fading. You passed up a chance to get to know someone. The environment is less personal now. People are no longer willing to bond.

Keyword: Love

Absent: The opportunity to be loving is missing. Your devotion is not encouraged. You can't show affection. Tender moments are few and far between. No one seems to care. Amorous overtures are being rebuffed.

Early Phase: You may have a chance to be loving. Someone may be more open to your advances in the future. A caring gesture may become necessary. An opportunity to forgive may come your way.

Late Phase: The opportunity to be loving is fading. Your attentions are no longer welcome. A chance to show caring has passed. Togetherness is ending. An apology is not easy now.

TWO OF CUPS

Upright

It's a time of connection and joining together. People are working as a unit. A marriage, union, or partnership is in the air. Truce is possible. You can forgive or be forgiven. An attraction exists. A bond is in place.

Reversed

Keyword: Connection

Absent: You're not connected right now. The marriage or other union is not happening. People are not seeing commonalties. Bonds are not being acknowledged. The group has failed to join together.

Early Phase: Connections may be forming. People may be coming together. Tentative links may be created. A marriage or other joining may be coming up. You may need to work with another person. Sharing may become an issue.

Late Phase: The connections are growing thin. There's less togetherness now. The links are dissolving. A marriage has taken place or is unraveling. Relationships are breaking up. You're no longer reaching out to someone.

Keyword: Truce

Absent: There's no truce at the moment. People are not speaking to each other. Opposites are far apart. Peace is not available now. Forgiveness is difficult. No agreement is happening.

Early Phase: Some peace overtures may be considered. A cease-fire may occur at some point. A truce may become possible. You're beginning to think about forgiveness. Warring parties may start coming together.

Late Phase: The truce is ending. Peaceful relationships are a thing of the past. The agreement is falling apart. Someone can't let bygones be bygones. Your ability to forgive is fading.

Keyword: Attraction

Absent: You don't feel attracted to someone. You can't generate a positive response. The proposal doesn't appeal to you. You're not inclined to move toward. You're reluctant to get drawn in.

Early Phase: An attraction may be developing. A bond may be forming. Someone or something may pull you in. You may feel more positive in the future.

Late Phase: An attraction is ending. It's hard to imagine what you saw in someone. You no longer feel positive about the matter. The appeal is fading. People have lost interest.

THREE OF CUPS

Upright

It's a time of exuberance and high spirits. Everyone is bursting with energy. Friendship is available. You can trust other people. A community exists. People are helping each other.

Reversed

Keyword: Exuberance

Absent: You're not feeling excited. The energy level is low. There's not much joy. People can't celebrate. The mood is damped down.

Early Phase: You may start to feel more energy. The mood may get lighter in the future. People may feel like celebrating one day. A joyous celebration may be approaching.

Late Phase: There's less excitement now. People are no longer exuberant. You're coming down from your high. The celebration is behind you. The dancing and singing are ending.

Keyword: Friendship

Absent: Friendship is lacking right now. You don't have anyone to confide in. You don't trust others at the moment. Someone is not being hospitable. There's little camaraderie right now.

Early Phase: There's a potential for friendship. You may get closer to an acquaintance. You may have to rely on a friend in the future. A chance to meet with friends may materialize.

Late Phase: A friendship is breaking up. You can no longer trust someone. There are fewer chances to meet with friends. Your buddies are less important to you now.

Keyword: Community

Absent: There's a lack of community. People are not helping each other. Neighbors are not friendly. Your support group is not available. The team spirit is low. The group bond is not strong.

Early Phase: A community may come together. A team spirit could develop in the future. You're thinking of joining with like-minded people. There's a potential for neighbors to get closer. Help may become available.

Late Phase: The community is breaking up. People are losing sight of a common goal. Neighbors are less friendly. You're leaving a support group or team. Bonds are no longer holding.

FOUR OF CUPS

Upright

It's a time of self-absorption. Personal concerns are primary. There's a mood of apathy and disengagement. Life seems stale and flat. You're going within. Introspection is important. Someone is withdrawing.

Reversed

Keyword: Self-absorption

Absent: There's a lack of self-absorption. People are not being selfish. Outsiders are not being forgotten. You aren't self-indulgent right now. You're ignoring your own needs at the moment.

Early Phase: You're thinking of focusing on yourself. You may begin to ignore others at some point. Someone could withhold affection in the future. Your areas of concern may start narrowing.

Late Phase: You're becoming less self-absorbed. You're no longer wrapped up in yourself. Egotistical behavior is decreasing. Personal concerns are taking a backseat.

Keyword: Apathy

Absent: Apathy is not evident. People are not losing interest. You're not feeling disengaged. There's no lack of caring. Someone is not being passive. Desire is not gone.

Early Phase: You may lose interest. Desire may disappear in the future. Someday you may not care as much. People may get bored at some point.

Late Phase: The apathy is going away. You're no longer disengaged. The lack of desire is fading. People are not so passive now. Someone is less uncaring.

Keyword: Going Within

Absent: It's impossible to focus within. You have little time for contemplation. Dreams are not being recognized. Your inner life is not flourishing. You don't trust your inner guidance.

Early Phase: You may start focusing on your inner life. Meditation and reflection could become important. Someone is thinking of withdrawing in the future. Vivid dreams may occur at some point.

Late Phase: Introspection is decreasing. You're having fewer dreams and inner experiences. There's less focus within. Someone is no longer hard to reach.

FIVE OF CUPS

Upright

It's a time of loss and sadness. Goodbyes are in the air. Someone or something is gone. Defeat is a reality. There's a mood of bereavement. A relationship is breaking up. You're feeling regret. A mistake is causing sorrow.

Reversed

Keyword: Loss

Absent: You're not experiencing loss. Nothing is being taken away. Someone is not saying goodbye. People are not losing hope. Defeat is not acknowledged. You're not accepting a loss.

Early Phase: You may experience a loss. Someone may leave in the future. A possession could become vulnerable. There's a potential for defeat. You may eventually lose hope.

Late Phase: The loss is behind you. You're dealing with a defeat. You experienced a setback. A theft has occurred. You've said your goodbyes. The letting go is ending.

Keyword: Bereavement

Absent: A relationship is not breaking up. You're not feeling alone. Abandonment is not an issue. Grief is not being expressed. A separation is not being acknowledged. Loved ones are not gone.

Early Phase: You could miss someone later. A loved one may depart in the future. A time of bereavement could occur. A mood of sadness may develop. You're thinking of a possible separation.

Late Phase: The period of bereavement is ending. You're no longer feeling sad. The loved one has departed. The loss of the relationship is behind you. You're feeling less deprived now.

Keyword: Regret

Absent: You're not feeling regret. There's little remorse. People are not sorry. Mistakes are not being acknowledged. You're not having second thoughts.

Early Phase: You may feel regret in the future. Someone may have second thoughts. An apology may become necessary. You may feel remorse some day. Tomorrow you may kick yourself.

Late Phase: You no longer feel regret. Remorse is decreasing. There's little point in crying over spilt milk. You have fewer reservations now.

SIX OF CUPS

Upright

It's a time of good will. People are sharing and offering support. Gifts are available. Innocence is an issue. Someone is unaware. Consciences are clear. There's a focus on childhood and play. A baby is involved.

Reversed

Keyword: Good Will

Absent: You're not experiencing good will. People are not kind and charitable. There's little sharing. A gift is not being offered. Noble impulses are not in evidence.

Early Phase: You may feel good will eventually. Someone could be generous in the future. Good intentions may exist at some point. There's a potential for sharing. A gift may be forthcoming.

Late Phase: Good will is decreasing. You're no longer feeling accommodating. There's less compassion now. The time for gifts is past. Help is less available now.

Keyword: Innocence

Absent: There's a lack of innocence. Someone's hands are not clean. You're not blind to what's going on. No one appreciates simple joys. An acquittal is not happening.

Early Phase: Innocence may be recognized. Your conscience may clear eventually. An acquittal may be approaching. Someone may be found blameless in the future.

Late Phase: The period of innocence is ending. You're no longer blissfully unaware. There's less resistance to corruption now. The desire to be good is fading. Someone was acquitted.

Keyword: Childhood

Absent: There's little focus on children. A baby or child is not in the picture. Someone is not feeling carefree. Chances to play are rare. You're ignoring childhood associations. Someone is not being taken care of.

Early Phase: A baby or child may become important. A pregnancy or birth could occur. You may get involved with children. There's a potential for play. Childhood memories may surface.

Late Phase: A pregnancy or birth has occurred. You're no longer focused on children. Playful moments are decreasing. Someone is acting less childish. A baby or child is becoming less central.

SEVEN OF CUPS

Upright

It's a time of wishful thinking. You have an elusive dream or hope. Options are available. You can pick and choose. Dissipation and excess are problems. There's a pattern of addiction.

Reversed

Keyword: Wishful Thinking

Absent: You're not kidding yourself. False illusions are not a problem. Your imagination is not running wild. Your idea is not a pipe-dream.

Early Phase: Wishful thinking could become a problem. You may lose touch with the truth at some point. Illusions may develop a life of their own. A fantasy could get stronger in the future.

Late Phase: You no longer believe in the dream. The bubble has burst. Hope is fading. The fantasy is less appealing now. You've let go of the illusion.

Keyword: Options

Absent: There are no options right now. The range of choices is limited. You can't afford to be choosy. You're refusing to look at alternatives. Someone is having trouble deciding.

Early Phase: Options may increase at some point. You could have more choices in the future. More possibilities may develop. Your vision could expand.

Late Phase: Your choices have narrowed. There are fewer options now. People can no longer pick and choose. Some possibilities have been removed. You eliminated some alternatives.

Keyword: Dissipation

Absent: You're not overindulging. Excess is being avoided. Laziness is not a problem. Someone is not procrastinating. Your health is not at risk. Addictions are not being acknowledged.

Early Phase: Laziness could become a problem. Loose living may start to be attractive. You could let everything go in the future. The environment could get disorganized. An addiction may develop.

Late Phase: The dissipation is ending. You're no longer overindulging. The addiction is coming under control. You're less disorganized now. The carousing is ending.

EIGHT OF CUPS

Upright

It's a time of deeper meaning. Values and personal truths are important. Someone is moving on. There's a need to disentangle. A journey is beginning. Weariness is a problem. People are burned out.

Reversed

Keyword: Deeper Meaning

Absent: The deeper meaning is not apparent. No one is looking for the truth. You're not concentrating on what's important. You're not avoiding the rat race. Your spirituality is being neglected.

Early Phase: You may start seeking deeper meaning. A hunger for truth could develop. A journey of discovery may begin in the future. Spiritual matters could become important. The atmosphere may turn serious.

Late Phase: You're less concerned with meaning now. Honest answers no longer matter. The serious tone is disappearing. People are forgetting what's important. Your spiritual yearnings are fading.

Keyword: Moving On

Absent: Someone is not moving on. You can't break free. Someone doesn't understand the need to let go. You can't leave a hopeless situation. Your trip is not getting off the ground.

Early Phase: You may need to move on in the future. The time to let go is approaching. Someone may decide to walk away. You're thinking of abandoning the situation.

Late Phase: Someone has moved on. You've removed yourself from the problem. A door has closed. You've said your goodbyes. A phase is ending. You no longer need to move on.

Keyword: Weariness

Absent: You're not tired right now. There's no lack of energy. Burn-out is not a problem. Demands are not too draining. You're not dragging through the day.

Early Phase: You could become fatigued. Someone may grow tired of the situation. Worry could consume you in the future. Burn-out may become an issue. A struggle may eventually wear you out.

Late Phase: Lack of energy is no longer a problem. The weight of the world has been lifted off your shoulders. You feel less tired now. The risk of burn-out is ending. The mood of resignation is lifting.

NINE OF CUPS

Upright

It's a time of wish fulfillment. You're achieving your heart's desire. Dreams are coming true. Satisfaction is yours. The situation is working out the way you want. Sensual pleasure is a delightful focus.

Reversed

Keyword: Wish Fulfillment

Absent: Your wish is not coming true. You're not getting what you think you want. Goals are being thwarted. Results don't match desires. The dream is not a reality.

Early Phase: You may realize your heart's desire. A goal could get closer. Someone's wish may be granted in the future. A prayer may be answered.

Late Phase: The time for getting your wish is past. You're no longer focused on a dream. Achieving your goal is less important now. Your desire is fading.

Keyword: Satisfaction

Absent: You're not satisfied. Results are not to your liking. Someone is put out. There's no pleasing some people. Contentment is low. You're not feeling smug right now.

Early Phase: You could become satisfied. The situation may get better. There's a potential for contentment. You may be pleased with your results in the future.

Late Phase: You're less satisfied now. The situation is no longer gratifying. Contentment is on the decline. Someone has upset the apple cart. People are not as smug as they were.

Keyword: Sensual Pleasure

Absent: You can't enjoy your senses. You have to forego pleasure. There are few opportunities to enjoy sex. Your body is constrained in some way. Beauty is not appreciated. Luxury is not an option. There's little focus on the arts.

Early Phase: You could begin seeking pleasure. A chance to enjoy your senses may come up. A sexual encounter may occur. You may have more luxury in the future.

Late Phase: Your focus on pleasure is decreasing. Sensual experiences are less common now. Sex is no longer as central. Surroundings are not as delightful. You can't afford to indulge at the same level.

TEN OF CUPS

Upright

It's a time of joy and good fortune. Emotional fulfillment is yours. Love is all around you. Happiness is available. Peace is in the air. The environment is calm. Family is important.

Reversed

Keyword: Joy

Absent: There is little joy right now. Happiness is elusive. You lack a sense of well-being. Someone can't express love openly. Good fortune is hard to come by.

Early Phase: You could feel joy. Moments of happiness may start to occur. There is potential for love. The future may be brighter. A more positive outlook could develop.

Late Phase: Your happiness is fading. There's less joy in the air. It's getting harder to count your blessings. The period of good fortune is past. Love is no longer strong.

Keyword: Peace

Absent: There's a lack of peace. The truce is broken. People are not friendly toward each other. Your serenity is disturbed. Someone is ill at ease. The environment is not harmonious.

Early Phase: A movement toward peace may start. An accord may become possible. Warring parties may begin talking. You may become more calm and relaxed. Harmony may return in the future.

Late Phase: The peace is ending. The time for reconciliation has passed. There's less desire for agreement now. The tranquil mood is evaporating. You're no longer responding calmly.

Keyword: Family

Absent: The family is disrupted. A family event is not going smoothly. A relative is having difficulty. Someone in the family is not included. Family members are not seeing eye-to-eye.

Early Phase: The family may come together. Family harmony may be possibile. A family matter may be resolved soon. A family celebration may be coming up.

Late Phase: Family togetherness is declining. Someone has shaken up the family. A family celebration has ended or was unable to occur. Family matters are becoming less important. You're no longer connected to your family.

PAGE OF CUPS

Upright

Cups' energy is available to help you move in a new direction. The call to be emotional, intuitive, intimate, and loving is strong right now. Take this chance to go beyond your usual limits and habits!

Reversed

Keywords: Be Emotional, Be Intuitive, Be Intimate, Be Loving

Absent: The time is NOT right, or you CAN'T follow the call to:

show your feelings, let your heart lead the way, express your sentiments, be moved, receive inner guidance, act on a hunch, trust your gut, sense the undercurrents, start or renew a love affair, get close to someone, go beyond formalities, move closer, forgive, respond with caring, avoid judgments, open your heart.

Early Phase: The time MAY BE APPROACHING when you'll have a chance to:

be romantic, shed detachment, cry or grieve, let the anger out, remember your dreams, pick up unspoken signals, be clairvoyant, trust your inner knowing, remove personal barriers, share something personal, make love, initiate sex, make a thoughtful gesture, feel sympathy, mend a broken relationship, hug.

Late Phase: The time is ENDING when you had a chance to:

feel joy, put feelings first, wear your heart on your sleeve, respond to beauty, be psychic, rely on guesses, read someone's mind, trust your sixth sense, provide confidential information, show warmth, share secrets, be personal, be understanding, show deep affection, turn away wrath, support unconditionally.

KNIGHT OF CUPS

Upright

Cups' energy is extra strong. You, someone else, or the situation may be romantic, imaginative, sensitive, refined, and introspective OR overemotional, fanciful, temperamental, over-refined, and introverted

Reversed

Keywords (Positive): Romantic, Imaginative, Sensitive, Overrefined
Keywords (Negative): Overemotional, Fanciful, Temperamental, Introverted

Absent: You or someone else is NOT:

> idealizing love, emphasizing emotions, showing imagination, sharing a vision, demonstrating deep caring, empathizing, honoring beauty, creating a pleasing environment, valuing the inner life, seeing into the heart OR showing jealousy, acting melodramatically, indulging in daydreams, shading the truth, experiencing mood swings, brooding, avoiding unpleasantness, getting overwhelmed, exaggerating failings, being driven to self-examination

Early Phase: You or another person MAY BEGIN to:

> enjoy the poetry of life, feel romantic, delve into the unconscious, avoid the ordinary, show sensitivity, be diplomatic, look for the finest, be more refined, seek self-improvement, try to understand OR be overemotional, blow hot and cold, let your imagination run wild, sulk, take offense easily, be finicky, focus on style over substance, be too introspective, become self-absorbed

Late Phase: You or another person is NO LONGER:

> remembering special moments, sharing feelings, using imagination, looking beyond the obvious, understanding another's pain, being discrete, acting with refinement, being gracious, looking within, being introspective OR being gushy, giving in to excess, indulging in fancies, focusing on big ideas that come to nothing, getting very depressed, being temperamental, being overly-fussy, leaving when the going gets rough, concerned only with self, obsessed with personal issues

QUEEN OF CUPS

Upright

Cups' energy is present as a state of being. A mood that is loving, tenderhearted, intuitive, psychic, and spiritual is evident. You or someone else is adopting or could adopt the mood of a lover, comforter, compassionate friend, psychic, intuitive, medium, spiritual guide, or minister.

Reversed

Keywords: Loving, Tenderhearted, Intuitive, Psychic, Spiritual

Absent: The mood of you or someone else is NOT:

> loving, accepting, sensitive, gentle, intuitive, guided by the heart, tuned-in, reverent, spiritual

Early Phase: The mood of you or someone else MAY BECOME:

> patient, caring, compassionate, kind, guided by trust, sympathetic, in-communion, devotional, ecstatic

Late Phase: The mood of you or someone else is NO LONGER:

> tender, affectionate, merciful, humane, solicitous, responsive, simpatico, devotional, joyful, blissful

KING OF CUPS

Upright

Cups' energy is present in an active, outgoing way. Actions that are wise, calm, diplomatic, caring, and tolerant are evident. You or someone else is acting or could act as a guide, counselor, healer, caring friend, wise teacher, caregiver, or mediator.

Reversed

Keywords: Wise, Calm, Diplomatic, Caring, Tolerant

Absent: You or someone else is NOT:

taking wise actions, giving good advice, calming tensions, keeping your head in a crisis, being tactful, diffusing a stressful situation, showing you care, helping someone in need, giving others their freedom, avoiding prejudice.

Early Phase: You or someone else MAY BEGIN to:

act with more awareness, demonstrate sound judgment, soothe ruffled feathers, provide a quieting influence, keep everyone together, mediate, provide healing, show compassion, accept limitations, respond patiently.

Late Phase: You or someone else is NO LONGER:

teaching wisely, helping constructively, staying composed, providing stability, staying balanced, showing diplomacy, volunteering, responding to a call for help, looking the other way, tolerating misdeeds.

ACE OF SWORDS

Upright

Swords' air energy is at your disposal right now. There's an opportunity to use mental force. You can expand your experience of fortitude, justice, and truth.

Reversed

Keyword: Mental Force

Absent: The opportunity to use mental force is missing. You lack an outlet for your intelligence. There's no chance to learn the facts. People are not being logical. Your ideas are not being heard.

Early Phase: You may have a chance to use mental force. You may be able to express your thoughts. Someone may become reasonable in the future. You may need to be more objective.

Late Phase: The opportunity to use mental force is fading. There are fewer intellectual challenges now. The chance to share your ideas is past. The time for thinking of a solution is ending. You no longer trust your analysis.

Keyword: Fortitude

Absent: The opportunity to show fortitude is missing. No one is letting you try. Your persistence is not appreciated. There's little adversity right now. Obstacles are few. People are not enduring.

Early Phase: You may have to show fortitude. Your resolve may be tested in the future. You may need to face your problems. An obstacle may be on the horizon. You may require inner strength.

Late Phase: The opportunity to show fortitude is fading. The test of your endurance is ending. The obstacle has been worked around. Setbacks are no longer a problem. The need for courage is no longer strong.

Keyword: Justice

Absent: The opportunity to be just is missing. You're not being treated fairly. No one supports your cause. People are not staying impartial. An equitable solution is not happening.

Early Phase: You may get a chance to be just. You may need to focus on what's fair. You could be offered an equal shot. Someone may try to make up for a past wrong. A matter of principle may come up.

Late Phase: The opportunity to be just is fading. You can no longer correct a mistake. The support for fair play is ending. You're less focused on doing what's right. Someone has revealed bias or prejudice.

Keyword: Truth

Absent: The opportunity to be truthful is missing. Honesty is not being encouraged. You're not allowed to say what you think. People can't let go of illusions. The facts are being ignored. You're resisting the urge to confess.

Early Phase: You may have a chance to be truthful. You could decide to be honest. Someone may open up to the facts. Your sincerity may be acknowledged. A revealing encounter may be coming up.

Late Phase: The opportunity to be truthful is fading. It's not as easy to be honest now. A chance to put everything on the table has passed. People no longer want to face reality. Someone has refused to confess.

TWO OF SWORDS

Upright

It's a time of blocked emotions. Feelings are being repressed. You're hiding some distress. Avoidance is a factor. People are choosing not to know. The situation is at a stalemate. Everyone is stuck.

Reversed

Keyword: Blocked Emotions

Absent: Emotions are not blocked at the moment. People are not hiding their feelings. Defenses are not working. It's hard to keep your distance. The usual restraints are not in place.

Early Phase: You may start shutting down emotionally. Your heart may become hardened. You're thinking of hiding your feelings. Walls may begin to form. Someone may become distant and cool.

Late Phase: You're unblocking your emotions. The ice is beginning to melt. Someone is less defensive now. You can no longer bottle up your feelings.

Keyword: Avoidance

Absent: You're not avoiding the truth. Pretending is not possible now. Choosing ignorance is not an option. People are not skirting the issues.

Early Phase: You may begin avoiding someone. Someone may start ignoring a problem. An unpleasantness may be swept under the rug. People may start pretending.

Late Phase: You can no longer avoid the situation. You've decided to stop pretending. People are less inclined to ignore the truth. It's no longer necessary to keep up a show.

Keyword: Stalemate

Absent: There's no stalemate at the moment. You're not stuck, despite appearances. A resolution is not out of the question. People are not afraid to act or make a decision.

Early Phase: A stalemate may develop. Positions may become fixed in place. Options may begin disappearing. You may be heading toward an impasse. It may get harder to maneuver in the future.

Late Phase: The stalemate is dissolving. People are no longer fixed in their positions. There's less fear of making a move. You're less reluctant to rock the boat.

THREE OF SWORDS

Upright

It's a time of heartbreak and disappointment. You or someone you know is hurting inside. Loneliness is a reality. You feel isolated from loved ones. Betrayal is in the air. A painful truth is being revealed.

Reversed

Keyword: Heartbreak

Absent: You're not suffering right now. No one's feelings are being hurt. There are no heartbreaking moments. The situation is not disappointing.

Early Phase: You may suffer pain in the future. You could be heading toward some heartbreak. You may begin feeling vulnerable emotionally. It's possible you could hurt someone in the future.

Late Phase: The heartbreak is behind you. The pain is dulling somewhat. You're coming to terms with your disappointment. You're no longer hurting someone.

Keyword: Loneliness

Absent: Loneliness is not a problem right now. You don't feel isolated or separated from others. There's no overt rejection. You haven't been deserted.

Early Phase: You may begin feeling lonely. A time of separation may be approaching. You may decide to reject someone, or be rejected. Your friends and loved ones may start pulling away.

Late Phase: You're no longer feeling lonely. Loved ones are less distant. A separation is ending. You're putting a rejection behind you. Isolation is becoming less of a problem.

Keyword: Betrayal

Absent: There's no betrayal for now. You're not being let down. The back-stabbing is not occurring. No one is taking actions against you at the moment.

Early Phase: You may begin feeling less trustful. You may be betrayed in the future. Someone may turn against you. You may start seeing signs of dishonesty. You're thinking of breaking your word or vows.

Late Phase: A betrayal has passed. The period of lying and deceit is ending. The painful revelations are behind you. You let someone down, but have resolved to mend your ways.

FOUR OF SWORDS

Upright

It's a time of rest and recovery. You can heal by enjoying peace and relaxation. Moments of contemplation are important. There is time to think and reflect. Quiet preparation for the future is vital.

Reversed

Keyword: Rest

Absent: There's no time for rest and relaxation. Peaceful moments are not available. You can't find the time for healing. You're not taking the breaks you need.

Early Phase: The pace may start to slow. You may need to take a break soon. A rest period may be approaching. You may have an opportunity to relax.

Late Phase: Your break period is ending. Your recovery is almost complete. The pace is no longer slow. Moments of peace and quiet are less frequent now.

Keyword: Contemplation

Absent: There's no time to think. People are not looking at the situation thoughtfully. You're not examining your motivations. No one is making an in-depth analysis.

Early Phase: A time for reflection may be approaching. You may need to stop and think things over. You could withdraw from the action for a time.

Late Phase: A period of contemplation is ending. You no longer need time alone to think. Your meditation is coming to an end. The thoughtful moments are decreasing.

Keyword: Quiet Preparation

Absent: No preparations are being made. There is no readiness. The situation is not stable. You're not in a position to handle whatever comes up.

Early Phase: You may begin preparations. Someone may be getting ready behind the scenes. You may need to secure your base in the future. Planning may become vital.

Late Phase: The preparation phase is over. You no longer need to secure the situation. You did what you needed to do. There's less focus on planning now.

FIVE OF SWORDS

Upright

It's a time of self-interest. People are putting their own needs first. There's a mood of hostility. Discord is evident. Everyone is taking sides. Open dishonor is a factor. Shady dealings are being exposed.

Reversed

Keyword: Self-Interest

Absent: You're not acting in your own self-interest. The mood is not openly selfish. No one is pushing a personal agenda. The needs of the group are not being ignored.

Early Phase: You may need to put yourself first. Selfishness may become more obvious. Someone may initiate a power play. A dog-eat-dog environment may develop.

Late Phase: There's less selfishness now. People are no longer self-absorbed. The blatant power plays are ending. The "me-first" mood is decreasing.

Keyword: Discord

Absent: There's no hostility at the moment. People are not fighting. The environment is not mean and nasty. People are not showing anger or ill-will.

Early Phase: The fighting may resume. A mood of ill-will may develop. The environment could get nasty. A battle may be brewing. You could become angry and out of sorts. People may start to take sides.

Late Phase: The conflict is ending. The environment is no longer openly hostile. The ill-will is fading. There's less anger and shouting. The biggest battle is behind you.

Keyword: Open Dishonor

Absent: There's no open dishonor. No criminal activity is going on. You're not losing sight of what's right. Integrity is not being sacrificed at the moment.

Early Phase: You may begin losing your moral compass. You're thinking of an illegal or unsavory act. Criminal activity may be exposed in the future. A test of integrity may be approaching. You could be tempted to take the low road.

Late Phase: A test of your integrity is behind you. Obvious dishonors are decreasing. You're no longer tempted to cheat. Criminal activity is in the past. The unsavory atmosphere is fading.

SIX OF SWORDS

Upright

It's time for the blues. Your energy and passion are low, but recovery is in progress. You're moving to a more positive place. Travel is a factor. A change of scene is in the air.

Reversed

Keyword: The Blues

Absent: You don't feel too sad or depressed. The blues are not a problem right now. You aren't feeling low or weighed down by concerns. You won't allow yourself to feel sad.

Early Phase: You may become depressed. You may be heading toward a low period. Life may begin losing its sparkle. You may need to face your sadness.

Late Phase: You're no longer sad. The mood of depression is lifting. You're putting the blues behind you. Your energy is returning. You're no longer discouraged.

Keyword: Recovery

Absent: You can't focus on recovery right now. You can't acknowledge the need to heal. People are not dealing with the aftermath of trauma. Coping mechanisms are not in place.

Early Phase: A time of healing may be approaching. You may have to focus on recovery. The after effects may become noticeable. You may begin mending.

Late Phase: The recovery period is ending. The healing process is behind you. The shock of the trauma is no longer as severe. Your convalescence is coming to an end.

Keyword: Travel

Absent: There's little travel. You're not moving to a new place. The current mood or scene is not changing. No one is being uprooted. A trip is not in the works.

Early Phase: You may have to leave on a trip. Someone may be planning a move. A change of scene may be coming up. An opportunity to travel may materialize. An inner journey may start.

Late Phase: You're returning from a trip. A move is behind you. You've taken an inner journey. A change of scene has been nearly completed. Travel is less likely now.

SEVEN OF SWORDS

Upright

Someone is leaving or running away. Responsibilities are being avoided. Procrastination is a problem. A lone-wolf style is in evidence. People are taking solitary actions. Hidden dishonors are a factor. There is dishonesty behind the scenes.

Reversed

Keyword: Running Away

Absent: No one is leaving. People are not taking the easy way out. There's little desire to sneak off. You're not shirking your obligations.

Early Phase: You're thinking about leaving. You may shirk a responsibility. Someone may try to sneak off. You may want to run away at some point.

Late Phase: You're no longer running away. The desire to escape is not so strong. There's less procrastination. Avoidance is decreasing.

Keyword: Lone-Wolf Style

Absent: You're unable to act on your own. Being solitary is not an option. You can't handle everything yourself. A lone-wolf style is not being encouraged.

Early Phase: You may need to be alone in the future. You're thinking of going solo. People may drift apart. A mood of alienation may develop. Independence may become attractive.

Late Phase: The lone wolf is rejoining the pack. People are no longer acting in isolation. Your desire for independence is fading. The need to stay apart is ending. Independent action is less acceptable now.

Keyword: Hidden Dishonor

Absent: There are no hidden dishonors at the moment. No one is deceiving or being deceived. People are not hiding shameful secrets. Undercover manipulations are not a factor.

Early Phase: You're thinking of doing something unworthy. You may head down a slippery slope. Someone may lie or cheat in the future. A crime or unpleasantness may be covered up.

Late Phase: Dishonorable acts are decreasing. You're extricating yourself from a dubious situation. You no longer want to live without integrity. You're putting the lies and cheating behind you. A shady past is less important now.

EIGHT OF SWORDS

Upright

It's a time of restriction and limitation. You're feeling trapped by circumstances. Few options seem available. There's confusion and lack of direction. No one's clear on the issues. Feelings of powerlessness are strong.

Reversed

Keyword: Restriction

Absent: You're not feeling restricted or tied down. There's no lack of options. No one is being persecuted. Obstacles are not a problem.

Early Phase: You may start feeling hemmed in. Restrictions may be put in place. There may be fewer choices in the future. Oppression may become a problem. The walls may begin closing in.

Late Phase: Restrictions are decreasing. You're feeling less confined. There are fewer obstacles in your way now. Oppression is ending. Freedom no longer seems impossible.

Keyword: Confusion

Absent: There's no uncertainty right now. People are not confused about what's happening. You're not feeling overwhelmed. Lack of direction is not a problem.

Early Phase: You may become uncertain. Confusion may increase. People could start floundering and lose purpose. Mixed messages may be sent at some point.

Late Phase: There's less uncertainty now. You no longer feel so overwhelmed. The period of confusion is behind you. Lack of direction is ceasing to be a problem.

Keyword: Powerlessness

Absent: You're not feeling victimized. Lack of power is not a factor. There's no need to seek rescue. Your hands are not tied.

Early Phase: You may lose power. Weakness could become a problem. People may start feeling vulnerable. Someone may become feeble or incapacitated.

Late Phase: You're no longer feeling like a victim. Doubts about your power are almost gone. Feelings of helplessness are fading. People are no longer immobilized.

NINE OF SWORDS

Upright

It's a time of worry and anxiety. Everyone is feeling tense. Feelings of guilt are strong. Someone is filled with regret. You're experiencing some anguish and moments of despair.

Reversed

Keyword: Worry

Absent: You have few misgivings about the situation. Worry is not a problem. There's little anxiety at the moment. There's no immediate cause for concern.

Early Phase: You may begin worrying. Some problems may preoccupy you in the future. You may have trouble sleeping. People could become apprehensive. Some anxious moments may be coming up.

Late Phase: You're worrying less now. The situation no longer seems troubling. Anxious moments are decreasing. Everyone seems less upset.

Keyword: Guilt

Absent: No one is guilty. There's little regret or remorse. Someone is not acknowledging guilt. You don't feel the need to punish yourself. Sin is not an issue.

Early Phase: You may feel guilty. You may have trouble forgiving yourself. Feelings of remorse may develop. You could experience regret in the future. Someone may be found guilty.

Late Phase: The guilt is decreasing. You're no longer being hard on yourself. There's less cause for regret now. The time for remorse is ending. A guilty verdict has been declared.

Keyword: Anguish

Absent: You're not depressed at the moment. The atmosphere is not gloomy. Despair is not being expressed. No one seems to be discouraged. You're not feeling despondent.

Early Phase: You may begin to despair. You may start crying more often. Painful memories could begin to surface. Someone may become depressed. The mood may get darker.

Late Phase: The anguish is fading. The dark times are behind you. The depression is lifting. You've been through a dark night of the soul.

TEN OF SWORDS

Upright

You're bottoming out. The situation is as bad as it's going to get. Victim mentality is a problem. You're feeling persecuted. Martyrdom is in the air. A sacrifice is being considered.

Reversed

Keyword: Bottoming Out

Absent: You haven't hit rock bottom. Matters are not hopeless. You're not allowing the worst to happen. Someone can't accept the seriousness of the situation.

Early Phase: A low period may be developing. Events may start going from bad to worse. You may enter a downward spiral. There may be some backsliding in the future.

Late Phase: The lowest point is behind you. You weathered the storm, and now the skies are clearing. You hit rock bottom, but managed to pull through. The discouraging signs are fading.

Keyword: Victim Mentality

Absent: You're not feeling like a victim. There are no signs of self-pity. Attacks are not occurring. People are not feeling persecuted. Loss of power is not a problem.

Early Phase: You may begin feeling like a victim. Someone may start indulging in self-pity. Attacks may become more frequent. You may suspect someone is targeting you. The victim role may become more central.

Late Phase: The situation seems less threatening. The attacks are decreasing. You're no longer on the receiving end. The period of powerlessness is ending.

Keyword: Martyrdom

Absent: There's no need to play the martyr. A sacrifice is not necessary. People are not letting themselves be walked on. The time is not right to make a stand.

Early Phase: You may start feeling like a doormat. Others could begin taking advantage. You may need to sacrifice in the future. Someone may be martyred for a principle. A mood of resignation may set in.

Late Phase: The martyr role is fading. You no longer need to put others first. The time of sacrifice is ending. There's less need to take a backseat now. The ordeal of suffering is behind you.

PAGE OF SWORDS

Upright

Swords' energy is available to help you move in a new direction. The call to use your mind, have fortitude, and be truthful and just is strong right now. The Page of Swords often represents a moment of challenge. Take this chance to go beyond your usual limits and habits!

Reversed

Keywords: Use Your Mind, Be Truthful, Be Just, Have Fortitude

Absent: The time is NOT right, or you CAN'T follow the call to:

> develop a plan, think clearly, get to the heart of the matter, analyze the situation, be honest, speak your mind, face the facts, avoid deceit, do what's fair, treat others equally, accept responsibility, right a wrong, keep your resolve, try repeatedly, hang tough, refuse to quit.

Early Phase: The time MAY BE APPROACHING when you'll have a chance to:

> be logical, examine your beliefs, do what's smart, out-think the other person, clear up confusion, give up lies, stop fooling yourself, admit there's a problem, act with principle, champion a cause, do what's right, accept the consequences, push past discouragement, get back on the horse, endure, outlast others.

Late Phase: The time is ENDING when you had a chance to:

> use your wits, figure out the solution, solve the puzzle, draw the right conclusions, be frank and open, stick to the facts, present an accurate picture, confess, stay impartial, avoid prejudice, honor fair play, stick to the law, be determined, show some spunk, test your mettle, stay firm.

KNIGHT OF SWORDS

Upright

Swords' energy is extra strong. You, someone else, or the situation may be direct, authoritative, incisive, knowledgeable, and logical OR blunt, overbearing, cutting, opinionated, and unfeeling.

Reversed

Keywords (Positive): Direct, Authoritative, Incisive/Cutting, Knowledgeable, Logical

Keywords (Negative): Blunt, Overbearing, Cutting, Opinionated, Unfeeling

Absent: You or someone else is NOT:

> being outspoken, getting right to the point, speaking with assurance, arguing a case forcefully, being incisive, demonstrating a keen intellect, becoming well-informed, finding out what's going on, using logic to good purpose, analyzing the situation OR speaking without tact, being brusque, becoming domineering, forcing a position on others, using too much sarcasm, being overly-critical, lacking tolerance, coming across as arrogant, treating people like numbers, staying too aloof.

Early Phase: You or another person MAY:

> speak your mind, be frank, command attention, act with certainty, get to the core issue, break through confusion, be sought as an expert, know the answers, reason clearly, set aside emotional factors OR be rude, disregard the feelings of others, expect immediate compliance, dominate the situation, be overbearing, indulge in put-downs, become close-minded, ignore other viewpoints, dismiss intuition, get cut off from feelings.

Late Phase: You or another person is NO LONGER:

> being straightforward, talking candidly, acting decisively, being a reliable source of information, expressing ideas succinctly, staying sharp and alert, staying knowledgeable, offering useful information, thinking rationally, being systematic OR being curt with others, wielding a sharp tongue, acting like a tyrant, squelching dissent, using a barbed wit, belittling associates, needing to have the last word, being dogmatic, ignoring suffering, acting cold and uncaring.

QUEEN OF SWORDS

Upright

Swords' energy is present as a state of being. A mood that is honest, astute, forthright, witty, and experienced is evident. You or someone else is adopting or could adopt the mood of a wit, comedian, trickster, con man, cynic, skeptic, whistle-blower, straight-shooter, coach, critic, or advisor.

Reversed

Keywords: Honest, Astute, Forthright, Witty, Experienced

Absent: The mood of you or someone else is NOT:

> honest, fair, smart. discerning, direct, straightforward, funny, clever, experienced, knowing.

Early Phase: The mood of you or someone else MAY BECOME:

> open, truthful, perceptive, insightful, frank, candid, playful, amusing, worldly, quick-on-the-uptake.

Late Phase: The mood of you or someone else is NO LONGER:

> realistic, authentic, clear-sighted, aware, plain-speaking, forthright, quick, sharp, cynical, jaded.

KING OF SWORDS

Upright

Swords' energy is present in an active, outgoing way. Actions that are intellectual, analytical, articulate, just, and ethical are important. You or someone else is acting or could act as a teacher, mentor, thinker, philosopher, theorizer, researcher, writer, translator, speaker, spokesperson, judge, or referee.

Reversed

Keywords: Intellectual, Analytical, Articulate, Just, Ethical

Absent: You or someone else is NOT:

    thinking carefully, grasping the concepts, acting rationally, arguing, communicating well, speaking with authority, staying objective, judging wisely, encouraging high standards, acting ethically

Early Phase: You or someone else MAY BEGIN to:

    conduct research, teach or learn, become involved in a game, apply logic, write, learn a language, tell the truth, take up a cause, shun corruption, take the high road

Late Phase: You or someone else is NO LONGER:

    using your mind, inspiring with ideas, dealing with complexity, analyzing the problem, articulating your position, telling it like it is, honoring all sides of an issue, doing what's fair, sticking to principles, acting honorably

ACE OF PENTACLES

Upright

Pentacles' earth energy is at your disposal right now. There's an opportunity to use material force. You can expand your experience of prosperity, practicality, and trust.

Reversed

Keyword: Material Force

Absent: The opportunity to use material force is missing. You lack a physical outlet. There's no chance to make a real-world impact. People are not focused on results. Your body or health is not strong.

Early Phase: You may have a chance to use material force. Physical strength may become necessary. Ideas could become more tangible. You may need to be more concrete. The natural world may become important.

Late Phase: The opportunity to use material force is fading. There are fewer physical challenges now. The chance to build something real is past. People are less interested in results. The environment is no longer being protected.

Keyword: Prosperity

Absent: The opportunity to be prosperous is missing. Chances to invest are lacking. Your efforts are not being rewarded. You're not reaching your stated goals. The environment is not conducive to growth.

Early Phase: You may have a chance for prosperity. A chance to invest may come up. The financial environment could improve in the future. Your assets may start to increase. You may get the support you need.

Late Phase: The opportunity to be prosperous is fading. An investment offer has been withdrawn. Chances to make money are no longer common. The climate of abundance is ending. Spending can't be as free now.

Keyword: Practicality

Absent: The opportunity to be practical is missing. Realistic plans are not being considered. No one is showing much common sense. You're not staying grounded. People are not focused on what will work.

Early Phase: You may have a chance to be practical. A realistic solution could materialize. You may need to focus on the tools at hand. Someone may become more down-to-earth. A real-world concern may come up.

Late Phase: The opportunity to be practical is fading. There's less support for the reasonable choice. Being sensible is no longer valued. The common sense approach is being discarded.

Keyword: Trust

Absent: The opportunity to trust or be trusted is missing. Someone is not telling the truth. You can't accept the situation at face value. Someone doesn't believe you. You can't prove your case. Confidences are not being kept.

Early Phase: You may have a chance to trust or be trusted. Someone may ask you to believe. Your reliability may be tested at some point. Someone may depend on you in the future.

Late Phase: The opportunity to trust or be trusted is fading. Someone no longer has faith in you. Your word is not good enough any more. Your desire to believe is nearly gone. You're not as gullible as you were.

TWO OF PENTACLES

Upright

It's a time of juggling. You must balance many demands. The situation is flexible and open to change. New directions are available. There is fun, laughter, and good times. All can be accomplished with great gusto.

Reversed

Keyword: Juggling

Absent: There's no need to juggle right now. You're not in a busy period. The pace is not hectic. Someone can't manage all the tasks. Balance is not being maintained.

Early Phase: There may be more demands in the future. A busy period may lie ahead. You may need to cover all the bases. Balance may become important.

Late Phase: The busy time is ending. You no longer have to struggle for balance. Demands were handled; now the pace is slowing. There's less need to juggle now.

Keyword: Flexible

Absent: The situation is not flexible. There's little openness to new approaches. You don't have room to maneuver. Someone is not adapting to changes.

Early Phase: There may be more flexibility in the future. You may be able to adapt. Someone may open to change. New options could develop at some point.

Late Phase: There's less flexibility now. You're no longer open to change. Your options are narrowing. The alternatives are disappearing.

Keyword: Fun

Absent: There's little fun right now. People are not enjoying themselves. You can't do what gives you pleasure. It's hard to see the humor in the situation.

Early Phase: A party or celebration may be coming up. You may have more fun in the future. There could be more opportunities for play. Good times may be on the way.

Late Phase: The fun is ending. People are no longer enjoying themselves. You have less time for play. A party or celebration has passed. The laughter is fading.

THREE OF PENTACLES

Upright

The time is right for teamwork. People are working together cooperatively. The focus is on planning and preparation. Competence is important. You're handling your tasks well. Everything is moving forward smoothly.

Reversed

Keyword: Teamwork

Absent: There's little teamwork. People are not functioning as a unit. Coordination is lacking. There's no spirit of cooperation. Someone refuses to join with others.

Early Phase: You may become part of a team. There's potential for cooperation. The group could come together in the future. A spirit of camaraderie may develop.

Late Phase: A team is breaking up. People are no longer functioning as a unit. Everyone is starting to go separate ways. There's less coordination and cooperation.

Keyword: Planning

Absent: There's no planning. People are not following a schedule. Preparations are lacking. You're not thinking about the future. No one is focused on what's to come.

Early Phase: You're thinking of making a plan. You may get organized at some point. The preparation stage may begin. A schedule could be implemented in the future.

Late Phase: There's less planning now. The schedule is slipping. The details are no longer being worked out. The preparation stage is ending. Your orderly projections are less reliable.

Keyword: Competence

Absent: Competence is lacking. The job is not being handled well. Goals are not getting met. You're not sure you can handle the situation successfully.

Early Phase: Someone may be more competent in the future. The system may start to work. People may begin handling their assignments better. You may find the skills you need.

Late Phase: The job is no longer getting done properly. Tasks are being neglected. You're losing confidence in your abilities. You have less faith in the system.

FOUR OF PENTACLES

Upright

It's a time of possessiveness. Issues of ownership are important. There's a mood of enforced stability. Someone is showing a need to control. You're blocking change or meeting resistance to change. Stagnation is a problem.

Reversed

Keyword: Possessiveness

Absent: There's little sense of ownership. Greed and jealousy are not a problem. You're not involved with staking claim or getting your share. You're denying a desire to possess.

Early Phase: You may become possessive. Jealousy or greed may develop. You may need to protect what you have. Someone may try to stake a claim.

Late Phase: You're less concerned with holding on. A focus on ownership is decreasing. There's no longer reason to be possessive. Jealousy is diminishing. People are less tied down.

Keyword: Control

Absent: There's no control. Few limits and restrictions are in place. The situation lacks direction. No one is keeping order. You have little structure in your life. There's no attempt to constrain you.

Early Phase: A need for order may develop. Limits and rules may become necessary. You could be asked to step in and take charge. There may be more structure in the future.

Late Phase: The structure in place is breaking up. Rules are no longer being followed. There is less control now. The level of organization is decreasing. You're losing your handle on the situation.

Keyword: Blocking Change

Absent: There are no blocks to change. Impediments do not exist. The way forward is not obscured. No obstacle is holding you back. No one is standing in your way.

Early Phase: A period of stagnation may be coming. Obstructions may occur. Resistance could become a problem. You may encounter roadblocks.

Late Phase: Blocks to change are decreasing. Resistance is fading. You're less opposed to new ideas and approaches. People are no longer committed to the status quo.

FIVE OF PENTACLES

Upright

Hard times are here. You're struggling with financial and practical problems. Ill health is a concern. Care of your body and its needs is important. Rejection or disapproval is an issue. Someone is being kept on the outside.

Reversed

Keyword: Hard Times

Absent: There's no lack of money. You're not having material problems. No one is in want right now. People do not need to struggle. Survival is not an issue.

Early Phase: Signs of financial trouble may develop. Hard times may be approaching. A period of lack could be on the horizon. You may feel insecure in the future.

Late Phase: The worse times are behind you. You no longer have to struggle so hard. There are fewer financial concerns. Practical problems are decreasing.

Keyword: Ill Health

Absent: Your health is not a problem right now. There are no symptoms at the moment. Sickness is not an issue. Someone is in remission. Your physical condition is not poor.

Early Phase: A health concern may develop in the future. A physical problem could show up. Your body may send you warning signs. You may start feeling weak. Stress and tension may become a problem.

Late Phase: The health crisis is behind you. A medical problem is less serious. You no longer feel run down and weak. Stress levels are decreasing. The symptoms are disappearing.

Keyword: Rejection

Absent: You're not being rejected. No one is being excluded. A dismissal is not happening. You don't have to rebuff someone. Refusal is not an option.

Early Phase: You may start seeing signs of disapproval. A rejection could occur in the future. Someone may refuse to go along. The door could be slammed in your face. Your proposal may be rebuffed.

Late Phase: Rejection is no longer an issue. You're feeling less excluded. The period of disapproval is behind you. You're no longer concerned with dismissal.

SIX OF PENTACLES

Upright

It's a time for issues of having/not having. You're involved with balancing resources, knowledge, or power. Questions of supply and demand are important.

Reversed

Keyword: Having/Not Having Resources

Absent: The distribution of resources is not a concern. You're not focused on getting more or having less. Who has what is not an issue. There's no need to think about supply.

Early Phase: You may have to think about resources in the future. You may need to take care of someone or be taken care of. A gift or reward may be offered. Issues of support may materialize.

Late Phase: There's less focus on resources. You no longer need to take care of someone or be taken care of. The time for a gift or reward is past. Support issues are decreasing.

Keyword: Having/Not Having Knowledge

Absent: The distribution of information is not a concern. You're not focused on what you know or don't know. You feel no need to offer or seek advice.

Early Phase: You may have to think about information in the future. You may start to teach or study. You may seek advice or be sought for your knowledge and opinion.

Late Phase: There's less focus on knowledge. The need to seek or offer advice is fading. You no longer want to teach or study. What people know is less important.

Keyword: Having/Not Having Power

Absent: The distribution of power is not a concern. You're not involved with who's in authority and who isn't. You're not coercing or being coerced.

Early Phase: You may have to think about power in the future. You may need to follow or lead. Issues of dominance and submission may become important.

Late Phase: There's less focus on power. The need to assert your authority or submit to someone is fading. Leadership issues are decreasing.

SEVEN OF PENTACLES

Upright

It's a time of assessment. You're taking stock of the situation. A reward is available. Your first efforts are bearing fruit. A direction change is in the air. A new path is worthy of consideration.

Reversed

Keyword: Assessment

Absent: No assessment is being made. There's no attempt to check results. You're not examining the situation closely. There's little time to pause and reflect.

Early Phase: You may need to evaluate. A status check may be coming up in the future. You may want to reassess where you're headed. A break may become necessary.

Late Phase: The assessment is ending. The time for evaluation is behind you. There's less need for thinking and planning. You no longer need to take stock of the situation.

Keyword: Reward

Absent: A reward is not materializing. There's no payoff at the moment. No sign of appreciation is appearing. You're not receiving your pat on the back.

Early Phase: A reward may be offered in the future. You may see some returns on your investment. A milestone may be coming up. A token of esteem may be presented.

Late Phase: The time for a reward has passed. Compensation is no longer available. The milestone is behind you. You've already received whatever was coming.

Keyword: Direction Change

Absent: A direction change is not happening. New opportunities are unavailable at the moment. You can't look at alternatives right now. A change of course is being blocked.

Early Phase: You may need a direction change in the future. Change may become more acceptable. A crossroads may be reached at some point. Someone may alter course.

Late Phase: The time for change is fading. The window of opportunity is closing. You're no longer weighing alternatives. A course adjustment is behind you.

EIGHT OF PENTACLES

Upright

It's a time of diligence. A great effort is being expended. A project is absorbing all your time. Knowledge is important. The information you want is available. You need to be careful and pay attention to detail.

Reversed

Keyword: Diligence

Absent: You're not working hard right now. A strong effort is not happening. You're not absorbed in a project. People are not industrious. No one is busy.

Early Phase: You may need to work harder in the future. A demanding project may be coming up. You may get involved in a new task. People may start gearing up for a big effort.

Late Phase: The hard work is behind you. You no longer need to work up a sweat. A project is winding down. Overtime is less available. You can slow down a bit.

Keyword: Knowledge

Absent: You're not pursuing knowledge. There's little opportunity to improve your skills. Research is not being done. You're having trouble getting the facts.

Early Phase: You may begin a course of study. You may need to increase your knowledge. School may become an option. An area of research may open up.

Late Phase: The time for study and learning is ending. A course is finishing up. Your knowledge is decreasing. The research is nearing completion. You found out what you needed to know.

Keyword: Detail

Absent: There's little attention to detail. Someone is not being careful. The necessary checking is not being done. You're not handling all the loose ends.

Early Phase: Details may become important. People could start being more methodical. The need for monitoring may become clear. Care may be required in the future.

Late Phase: Extra care is no longer required. The need to check and double-check is past. You're less painstaking now. The detail work is ending.

NINE OF PENTACLES

Upright

It's a time of discipline. You need to control impulses and show restraint. Self-reliance is important. You can handle matters by yourself. An environment of refinement and gracious living is possible.

Reversed

Keyword: Discipline

Absent: There's little discipline at the moment. You're not sticking to the program. Wayward impulses are not being controlled. There's a lack of restraint.

Early Phase: You may need more discipline in the future. Self-control may become important. Someone may have to be restrained. A firm hand may be necessary.

Late Phase: Discipline is breaking down. Control measures are no longer in place. You're abandoning the program. People are less rigorous now. The regimen is no longer being followed.

Keyword: Self-Reliance

Absent: You can't act on your own. Your desire for independence is blocked. You can't handle the situation alone. Someone is not self-sufficient.

Early Phase: You're thinking of becoming more independent. You may be on your own in the future. Someone may become more self-reliant. You may need to break away at some point.

Late Phase: It's no longer possible to do everything yourself. A period of independence is ending. Being on your own is less satisfying now. The need for self-reliance is no longer strong.

Keyword: Refinement

Absent: There's a lack of refinement. People are not being tactful and polite. You're missing the finer things of life right now. Someone is refusing to be gracious.

Early Phase: People may become more courteous. You may seek more refined activities in the future. The environment may become more pleasant. There's potential for gracious living.

Late Phase: People are no longer cordial. The gracious environment is disappearing. You're less interested in refined activities now. The gloves are coming off.

TEN OF PENTACLES

Upright

It's a time of affluence. All ventures are flourishing. Permanence is
important. A lasting foundation is being established. People are following
convention. There's a need to comply with rules and guidelines.

Reversed

Keyword: Affluence

Absent: You're not enjoying abundance right now. Financial success is elusive. You can't seem to
   get projects off the ground. Good fortune is lacking.

Early Phase: Your fortunes may improve in the future. Your financial situation could get better.
   Business may pick up. Some prospects may develop.

Late Phase: Your run of good fortune is ending. The prosperous times have passed. You're no
   longer feeling financially secure. Business has taken a turn for the worse.

Keyword: Permanence

Absent: You can't find a permanent solution. There's no solid base in place. No one is focused on
   the long term. The family is not settled and secure.

Early Phase: You may seek a long-term solution. A more permanent foundation may materialize.
   You may be able to settle down. A secure relationship may become more appealing.

Late Phase: Your fixed arrangement is falling apart. You're no longer focused on making the
   situation last. The mood of security is disappearing. A long-lasting relationship is ending.

Keyword: Convention

Absent: There's little concern with convention. Traditions are not being followed. You don't trust
   the standard approach. Someone is not playing by the rules.

Early Phase: You may become more conservative. Rules may need to be followed. Someone may
   decide to go along with convention. A tradition may be honored.

Late Phase: You're no longer following a tradition. The mood is becoming less conventional.
   Known patterns are less effective. People are growing disenchanted with the old ways.

PAGE OF PENTACLES

Upright

Pentacles' energy is available to help you move in a new direction. The call to have an effect or be practical, prosperous, trusting, and trustworthy is strong right now. Take this chance to go beyond your usual limits and habits!

Reversed

Keywords: Have an Effect, Be Practical, Be Prosperous, Be Trusting/Trustworthy

Absent: The time is NOT right, or you CAN'T follow the call to:

> put plans into motion, get heard, make physical changes, alter course, find a solution that works, use common sense, take advantage of what's available, get real, enrich yourself, enjoy abundance, reap rewards, make your fortune, keep your word, accept others at their word, stick by commitments, be credible.

Early Phase: The time MAY BE APPROACHING when you'll have a chance to:

> achieve results, make a difference, set events in motion, realize your dream, work with what you have, be sensible, do what's necessary, accept reality, become secure, see your efforts flourish, attract you what you need, find the means, be dependable, have faith in someone, let go of the need to control, keep a promise.

Late Phase: The time is ENDING when you had a chance to:

> work materially, take action, make an impression , apply pressure, solve a problem, be pragmatic, show good judgment, do what it takes, enjoy success, grow and expand, thrive, be comfortable, keep believing, stay loyal, honor your vow, stick to the agreement.

KNIGHT OF PENTACLES

Upright

Pentacles' energy is extra strong. You, someone else, or the situation may be unwavering, cautious, thorough, realistic, and hardworking OR stubborn, unadventurous, obsessive, pessimistic, and grinding.

Reversed

Keywords (Positive): Unwavering, Cautious, Thorough, Realistic, Hardworking

Keywords (Negative): Stubborn, Unadventurous, Obsessive, Pessimistic, Grinding

Absent: You or someone else is NOT:

standing firm against opposition, staying true to convictions, showing caution, taking the prudent path, being thorough, covering all bases, facing the truth squarely, anticipating problems honestly, working hard, putting in a good effort OR being stubborn, refusing to listen to reason, being too conservative, settling for what's safe, being too picky, insisting on perfection, taking the gloomy view, dooming a project from the start, being humorless, driving others too hard.

Early Phase: You or another person MAY BEGIN to:

stay fixed to a course, be unwavering, check and double-check, proceed slowly, be meticulous, wrap up all loose ends, be willing to look at the facts, accept what's practical, tackle what needs doing, be industrious OR resist compromise, dig into a position, be overly-cautious, stay stuck in a rut, become obsessive, demand that everything be just so, be too pessimistic, concentrate on what's wrong, focus too much on work, forget about fun.

Late Phase: You or another person is NO LONGER:

refusing to quit, hanging in there, being careful, keeping your eyes open, seeing the job through, taking care of the details, keeping feet on the ground, staying in the realm of possibility, staying productive, sticking to it OR impossible to budge, insisting on having his/her way, being a stick-in-the-mud, afraid to risk, nagging, being too compulsive, seeing the glass as half-empty, focusing on the worst case, being a grind, cracking the whip.

QUEEN OF PENTACLES

Upright

Pentacles' energy is present as a state of being. A mood that is nurturing, big-hearted, down-to-earth, resourceful, and trustworthy is evident. You or someone else is adopting or could adopt the mood of a parent, guardian, caretaker, nurturer, healer, friend, volunteer, resource-person, confidante, or right-hand man.

Reversed

Keywords: Nurturing, Bighearted, Down-to-Earth, Resourceful, Trustworthy

Absent: The mood of you or someone else is NOT:

> supportive, nurturing, giving, generous, matter-of-fact, sensible, practical, handy, versatile, loyal, reliable.

Early Phase: The mood of you or someone else MAY BECOME:

> warm, natural, welcoming, abundant, unpretentious, simple, resourceful, ingenious, steadfast, trustworthy.

Late Phase: The mood of you or someone else is NO LONGER:

> loving in a practical way, sustaining, free of selfishness, bighearted, earthy, easygoing, pragmatic, workable, confidential, faithful.

KING OF PENTACLES

Upright

Pentacles' energy is present in an active, outgoing way. Actions that are enterprising, adept, reliable, supporting, and steady are evident. You or someone else is acting or could act as a businessperson, entrepreneur, manager, deal-maker, problem-solver, craftsperson, artisan, provider, philanthropist, or source of strength.

Reversed

Keywords: Enterprising, Adept, Reliable, Supporting, Steady

Absent: You or someone else is NOT:

enterprising, attracting wealth, showing competence, using skills, meeting commitments, assuming responsibility, offering to help, providing support, remaining constant, keeping regular habits.

Early Phase: You or someone else MAY BEGIN to:

make something work, solve the problem, prove adept, focus on what's practical, keep promises, stay reliable, give generously, encourage someone, provide stability, work steadily toward a goal.

Late Phase: You or someone else is NO LONGER:

picking up on opportunities, taking care of business, managing well, relying on experts, instilling trust, following through, giving time and attention, propping up, staying calm, avoiding mood swings.

SUGGESTIONS FOR EXERCISES

These suggestions are examples of possible responses to some of the exercises. They're not answers; they are simply samples of the kinds of insights you can get from the cards. In the tarot, whatever your intuition tells you is valid. Everyone sees the world through a different lens. Your goal is to learn how your particular lens works.

LESSON TWO:
THE ENERGY CYCLE AND ORIENTATION

Suggestions for Exercise 2.2: Is the Energy Present or Lacking?

1. Fitness is actively present—upright
2. Depression is actively present—upright
3. Compassion is lacking—reversed
4. Greed is lacking—reversed
5. Pride is actively present—upright
6. Attraction is lacking—reversed
7. Sorrow is lacking—reversed
8. Devotion is actively present—upright
9. Creativity is lacking—reversed
10. Denial is lacking—reversed

Suggestions for Exercise 2.3: Lacking vs. Opposing Energies

1.
   #1 = lacking (not very enthusiastic)
   #2 = opposite (rejecting, opposing, dismissing)
2.
   #1 = opposite (dependent, bound to others)
   #2 = lacking (not too self-reliant)
3.
   #1 = lacking (not honest)
   #2 = opposite (dishonest, deceitful, false)
4.
   #1 = lacking (not yet practical)
   #2 = opposite (crazy, impractical, fanciful)
5.
   #1 = lacking (not very funny)
   #2 = opposite (sad, heartbreaking, tragic)
6.
   #1 = opposite (failing, losing, going under)
   #2 = lacking (not achieving much)

7.
   #1 = opposite (selfish, egotistical)
   #2 = lacking (not ready to sacrifice)

8.
   #1 = lacking (not running away for now)
   #2 = opposite (committed, engaged, bonded)

9.
   #1 = opposite (energized, robust, vigorous)
   #2 = lacking (not so tired)

10.
   #1 = opposite (literal, specific, cut-and-dried)
   #2 = lacking (not very imaginative)

LESSON THREE: ENERGY PHASES

Suggestions for Exercise 3.1: Which Phase?

1. Late phase—reversed
   The test is almost over for you when you turn in your exam.
2. Early phase—reversed
   The opening scene of a movie is in the early phase of the film.
3. Late phase—reversed
   Goodbye means your visit is almost over.
4. Middle phase—upright
   Giving your speech is the peak moment your preparations were leading to.
5. Early phase—reversed
   The first day of school is the start of the school year.
6. Middle phase—upright
   Reaching the top is the "peak" of your climb.
   (A mountain's shape matches the energy curve.)
7. Late phase—reversed
   Your vacation is ending when you arrive home.
8. Early phase—reversed
   Spring is the early phase of the growing season in your garden.
9. Middle phase—upright
   The main course comes in the middle and is the highlight of the meal (unless you love dessert).
10. Middle phase—upright, **or** early phase—reversed
   Exchanging vows is the peak moment of the wedding ceremony (middle phase—upright), but it also marks the beginning of the marriage (early phase—reversed). The choice depends on which energy you're focusing on.

Suggestions for Exercise 3.2: Is the Energy Growing or Fading?

1. Relationship is decreasing—Lovers
2. Restriction is increasing—Eight of Swords
3. Prosperity is increasing—Ten of Pentacles

4. Diligence is increasing—Eight of Pentacles

5. Hope is increasing—Star

6. Truce is decreasing—Two of Cups

7. Trust is decreasing—Queen of Pentacles

8. Apathy is increasing—Four of Cups

9. Competence is increasing—Three of Pentacles

10. Downfall is decreasing—Tower

Suggestions for Exercise 3.3: Which Card Fits?

1. a. Upright Six of Wands

   The energy of triumph is at its maximum strength.

2. b. Reversed Queen of Swords

   The energy of honesty and directness is absent.

3. a. Reversed Ten of Cups

   The desire to contact the family isn't developed.

4. b. Reversed Tower

   The disruption of the Tower is in the past (late phase). Death also represents a major transition, but Death is upright, implying the crisis is still in effect.

5. b. Upright Empress

   The energy of mothering is strong, but a new baby can also require fortitude (Page of Swords) and hard work (Ten of Wands)!

6. c. Reversed Ace of Cups

   There's an opportunity coming up to meet a love interest (early phase).

7. c. Reversed Knight of Pentacles

   The obsessive editor has left (late phase). The Knight of Swords is hyper-critical too, but an upright card suggests someone still active.

8. b. Reversed Seven of Pentacles

   The chance for a direction change is no longer strong (late phase).

9. a. Upright Three of Swords

   The energy of loneliness is strong and immediate (middle phase).

10. a, b, and c

    There is always overlap in the tarot. Each choice fits the energy of this statement in some way. The reversed Eight of Wands implies not facing some news. The upright Two of Swords and upright Seven of Swords both suggest full-blown avoidance.

LESSON FOUR: REPEATING CYCLES

Exercise 4.1: New or Repeating Energy?

1. Energy of trust = repeating
   Possible past assumptions:
      She always lies.
      I'd be a fool to trust her again.
      I was sorry the last time I trusted.
2. Energy of realizing your dream = new
   No assumptions from the past
3. Energy of financial security = new
   No assumptions from the past
4. Energy of feeling like a victim = new
   No assumptions from the past
5. Energy of fun = repeating
   Possible past assumptions:
      The resort is always a fun place.
      The upcoming event will be like earlier ones.
      It's great to have fun.
6. Energy of confidence = repeating
   Possible past assumptions:
      I can't stay confident.
      I run into problems when I get too sure of myself.
      I always mess up somehow.
7. Energy of organization = new
   No assumptions from the past
8. Energy of hidden dishonor = repeating
   Possible past assumptions:
      I'm helpless in this situation.
      My job's at stake.
      It's wrong, but nothing happened last time.

9. Energy of letting go = new

No assumptions from the past

10. Energy of forgiveness = repeating

Possible past assumptions:

He expects me to forgive as I always do.

I always give in if I talk to him.

He's hasn't changed.

Note: Even though the energy is repeating, the response is new!

Exercise 4.2: Complete or Incomplete Energy?

1. Energy of rest and recovery = complete

The rest period is over and it's time to be busy again.

2. Energy of prosperity = complete

The sale is over, so it's back to business as usual.

3. Energy of wishful thinking = incomplete

The fantasy has been recognized for what is was, but it still holds some power.

4. Energy of mystery = incomplete

The mystery is not really resolved until you're satisfied it is.

5. Energy of friendship = complete

The meeting with friends was complete in itself. No unresolved issues linger.

6. Energy of fear = incomplete

The fear is gone, but it's likely to come back.

7. Energy of courage = complete

The sky dive was a one-time, satisfying experience.

8. Energy of hard control = complete

Hard control has been abandoned for a more effective approach.

9. Energy of sexuality = incomplete

The issue of sex in the relationship has not been resolved.

10. Energy of love = incomplete

Love is not present now, but it's still hoped for.

LESSON FIVE: MISMATCHES

Exercise 5.1: Actuality vs. Belief

1.

Travel is actually high (card is upright).

Travel is believed to be high (traveling all the time).

Match

2.

Aggression is actually strong (card is upright).

Aggression is believed to be low (I'm not really mad).

No match

Misperception = There's more anger than is acknowledged.

3.

Attention to detail is actually low (card is reversed).

Attention to detail is believed to be high (checked ten times).

No match

Misperception = The checking was not as thorough as it seemed.

4.

Romance is actually low (card is reversed).

Romance is believed to be low (few romantic moments).

Match

5.

Moderation is actually low (card is reversed).

Moderation is believed to be high (quiet, moderate life).

No match

Misperception = There's more overindulgence than there seems.

6.

Recognition is actually high (card is upright).

Recognition is believed to be low (I've been forgotten).

No match

Misperception = People do remember.

7.

    Quiet contemplation is actually low (card is reversed).

    Quiet contemplation is believed to be low (little meditation).

    Match

8.

    Leadership is actually low (card is reversed).

    Leadership is believed to be high (I'm a good leader).

    No match

    Misperception = The team may not respect the leadership after all.

9.

    Fairness is actually high (card is upright).

    Fairness is believed to be high (reputation for fairness).

    Match

10.

    Attraction is actually high (card is upright).

    Attraction is believed to be low (He's not attracted).

    No match

    Misperception = He's more interested than he seems.

LESSON SIX:
OPPOSING ENERGY PAIRS

Exercise 6.1: Matching Opposing Pairs

Enthusiasm, Apathy/Four of Wands, Four of Cups

Resting, Quick Action/Four of Swords, Eight of Wands

Mother, Father/Empress, Emperor

Materiality, Spirit/Ace of Pentacles, Ace of Cups

Hope, Hopelessness/Star, Devil

Solitude, Relationship/Hermit, Lovers

Guilt, Innocence/Nine of Swords, Six of Cups

Vitality, Weariness/Sun, Eight of Cups

Winning, Losing/Six of Wands, Five of Cups

Originality, Convention/Two of Wands, Ten of Pentacles

Exercise 6.2: Interpreting Opposing Pairs

1. Two approaches are evident in the situation. One comes from analysis, logic, and reason (high level of mental force). The other is more emotional and intuitive (high level of emotional force).

2. Right now the situation is structured (upright Four of Pentacles), but there's a chance everything will dissipate and fall apart (reversed early phase Seven of Cups.)

   The situation was loose and out of control, but not any more (reversed late phase Seven of Cups). Controls have been put in place to provide needed structure. (upright Four of Pentacles).

3. Right now no actions are being taken (upright High Priestess), but that may not last. There's a growing urge to take action (reversed early phase Magician.)

   Some action was taken (reversed late phase Magician) in the past, and now everyone is waiting to see what will develop (upright High Priestess).

4. Sometimes life is fun (Two of Pentacles), sometimes it's not (Six of Swords). There are these mood shifts, but neither feeling has a firm hold yet (reversed).

5. Someone is determined to look ahead and make realistic plans for the future (upright Three of Wands). Someone else is equally firm about avoiding all future planning (upright Two of Swords).

6. Both parties are looking for control in the situation. One is trying to take over by strength of will (upright Chariot). The other is more subtle, using persuasion and soft control methods (upright Strength).

7. One person is trying to hold the fort alone (upright Nine of Pentacles), but the cavalry is on the way (reversed early-phase Three of Pentacles.)

   The team was working well together, but no more (reversed late-phase Three of Pentacles). The harmony was disrupted when one member decided to act alone (upright Nine of Pentacles).

8. Times are hard at the moment (upright Five of Pentacles), but the chance for greater abundance and material comfort may be approaching (reversed early-phase Empress).

   A time of plenty was enjoyed for a time (reversed late-phase Empress), it's ending. Now there's a struggle to make ends meet (upright Five of Pentacles).

9. A relationship has a low energy level at the moment (reversed). It lacks moments of joy (Ten of Cups), but also peak moments of heartache (Three of Swords).

10. The present seems dominated by burdens and cares (upright Ten of Wands). A strong need to have some carefree, spontaneous moments is asserting itself (reversed early-phase Fool.)

    There was a good period of carefree living, but that's all over (reversed late-phase Fool). It's been replaced by some burdensome issues that must be taken care of (upright Ten of Wands).

    Note: The Fool energy may be low, but it's stronger than it seems because the Fool is a major arcana card.

CARD KEYWORD LIST

Major Arcana

The Fool: Beginning, Spontaneity, Faith, Apparent Folly

The Magician: Action, Conscious Awareness, Concentration, Power

The High Priestess: Nonaction,Unconscious Awareness, Potential, Mystery

The Empress: Mothering, Abundance, Senses, Nature

The Emperor: Fathering, Structure, Authority, Regulation

The Hierophant: Education, Belief Systems, Conformity, Group Identification

The Lovers: Relationship, Sexuality, Personal Beliefs, Values

The Chariot: Victory, Will, Self-Assertion, Hard Control

Strength: Strength, Patience, Compassion, Soft Control

The Hermit: Introspection, Searching, Guidance, Solitude

Wheel of Fortune: Destiny, Turning Point, Movement, Personal Vision

Justice: Justice, Responsibility, Decision, Cause and Effect

The Hanged Man: Letting Go, Reversal, Suspension, Sacrifice

Death: Ending, Transition, Elimination, Inexorable Forces

Temperance: Temperance, Balance, Health, Combination

The Devil: Bondage, Materialism, Ignorance, Hopelessness

The Tower: Sudden Change, Release, Downfall, Revelation

The Star: Hope, Inspiration, Generosity, Serenity

The Moon: Fear, Illusion, Imagination, Bewilderment

The Sun: Enlightenment, Greatness, Vitality, Assurance

Judgement: Judgment, Rebirth, Inner Calling, Absolution

The World: Integration, Accomplishment, Involvement, Fulfillment

Minor Arcana and Court Cards

Wands

Ace of Wands: Creative Force, Enthusiasm, Confidence, Courage

Two of Wands: Personal Power, Boldness, Originality

Three of Wands: Exploration, Foresight, Leadership

Four of Wands: Celebration, Freedom, Excitement

Five of Wands: Disagreement, Competition, Hassles

Six of Wands: Triumph, Acclaim, Pride

Seven of Wands: Aggression, Defiance, Conviction

Eight of Wands: Quick Action, Conclusion, News

Nine of Wands: Defensiveness, Perseverance, Stamina

Ten of Wands: Overextending, Burdens, Struggle

Page of Wands: Be Creative, Be Enthusiastic, Be Courageous, Be Confident

Knight of Wands (Positive): Charming, Self-Confident, Daring, Adventurous, Passionate

Knight of Wands (Negative): Superficial, Cocky, Foolhardy, Restless, Hot-Tempered

Queen of Wands: Attractive, Wholehearted, Energetic, Cheerful, Self-Assured

King of Wands: Creative, Inspiring, Forceful, Charismatic, Bold

Cups

Ace of Cups: Emotional Force, Intuition, Intimacy, Love

Two of Cups: Connection, Truce, Attraction

Three of Cups: Exuberance, Friendship, Community

Four of Cups: Self-Absorption, Apathy, Going Within

Five of Cups: Loss, Bereavement, Regret

Six of Cups: Good Will, Innocence, Childhood

Seven of Cups: Wishful Thinking, Options, Dissipation

Eight of Cups: Deeper Meaning, Moving On, Weariness

Nine of Cups: Wish Fulfillment, Satisfaction, Sensual Pleasure

Ten of Cups: Joy, Peace, Family

Page of Cups: Be Emotional, Be Intuitive, Be Intimate, Be Loving

Knight of Cups (Positive): Romantic, Imaginative, Sensitive, Refined, Introspective

Knight of Cups (Negative): Overemotional, Fanciful, Temperamental, Overrefined, Introverted

Queen of Cups: Loving, Tenderhearted, Intuitive, Psychic, Spiritual

King of Cups: Wise, Calm, Diplomatic, Caring, Tolerant

Swords

Ace of Swords: Mental Force, Fortitude, Truth, Justice,

Two of Swords: Blocked Emotions, Avoidance, Stalemate

Three of Swords: Heartbreak, Loneliness, Betrayal

Four of Swords: Rest, Contemplation, Quiet Preparation

Five of Swords: Self-Interest, Discord, Open Dishonor

Six of Swords: The Blues, Recovery, Travel

Seven of Swords: Running Away, Lone-Wolf Style, Hidden Dishonor

Eight of Swords: Restriction, Confusion, Powerlessness

Nine of Swords: Worry, Guilt, Anguish

Ten of Swords: Bottoming Out, Victim Mentality, Martyrdom

Page of Swords: Use Your Mind, Be Truthful, Be Just, Have Fortitude

Knight of Swords (Positive): Direct, Authoritative, Incisive, Knowledgeable, Logical

Knight of Swords (Negative): Blunt, Overbearing, Cutting, Opinionated, Unfeeling

Queen of Swords: Honest, Astute, Forthright, Witty, Experienced

King of Swords: Intellectual, Analytical, Articulate, Just, Ethical

Pentacles

Ace of Pentacles: Material Force, Prosperity, Practicality, Trust

Two of Pentacles: Juggling, Flexibility, Fun

Three of Pentacles: Teamwork, Planning, Competence

Four of Pentacles: Possessiveness, Control, Blocked Change

Five of Pentacles: Hard Times, Ill Health, Rejection

Six of Pentacles: Having/Not Having, Resources, Knowledge, Power

Seven of Pentacles: Assessment, Reward, Direction Change

Eight of Pentacles: Diligence, Knowledge, Detail

Nine of Pentacles: Discipline, Self-Reliance, Refinement

Ten of Pentacles: Affluence, Permanence, Convention

Page of Pentacles: Have an Effect, Be Practical, Be Prosperous, Be Trusting/Trustworthy

Knight of Pentacles (Positive): Unwavering, Cautious, Thorough, Realistic, Hardworking

Knight of Pentacles (Negative): Stubborn, Unadventurous, Obsessive, Pessimistic, Grinding

Queen of Pentacles: Nurturing, Bighearted, Down-to-Earth, Resourceful, Trustworthy

King of Pentacles: Enterprising, Adept, Reliable, Supporting, Steady